Guide to
Letter
Writing

Betty Kirkpatrick

BROCKHAMPTON PRESS
LONDON

This edition published 1996 by Brockhampton Press, a member of the
Hodder Headline PLC Group

ISBN 1 86019 390 0

Printed and bound in India

Contents

Chapter 1

The Decline of the Letter

The mass introduction of the telephone dealt what was almost a mortal blow to the art of letter-writing. By the second part of the twentieth century all but the most poverty-stricken households in Britain had a telephone installed and those who did not have access to one in the home could use a public telephone booth—if they could find one that had not been vandalized.

The telephone has many obvious advantages over letter-writing apart from the fact that it is considerably less common to have an unintelligible voice than it is to have illegible handwriting. It is a far more immediate form of communication in that the response is instant and an exchange of views can take place on the spot. In the case of a letter, time has to be allowed for the letter to reach the person written to, and time allowed for the reply to return, not to mention the time taken for the rely to be mulled over and written. Then allowance has to be made for procrastination, such as the time during which the original letter lies in the recipient's in-tray.

Another obvious advantage that the telephone has over the letter is that you can be absolutely certain that your message has reached the person for whom it is intended. Despite the vociferous criticism it receives, our postal service is for the most part reasonably reliable, although there is always the odd letter that goes astray, and the slightly more frequent letter that gets delayed. Valuable time can be wasted while you are wondering whether the letter has got to its destination, whether the reply is on its way or whether the delay is simply a matter of apathy on the part of your correspondent. Of course, in these modern times the fax, about which information is given later in the chapter, is supposed to have removed this disadvantage from the written word.

The telephone has a more informal, personal advantage as well. If the person at the other end of the telephone line is a lover, good friend or family member, there is the pleasure of hearing his or her voice, a pleasure that is particularly welcome if the person lives far away and is rarely present in person. If a face-to-face chat is not a possibility, the next best thing is a phone-to-phone one.

These advantages are greatly appreciated by most of us. If we are truthful, however, we would probably have to admit that what we really appreciate most about the telephone is that it saves us a good deal of effort. If the telephone call is an important one, however, we may have to spend some time thinking out what we are going to say, although this will still require considerably less time, effort and organization than writing a letter.

The telephone does not have it all its own way and the letter still has several advantages. Not least, in these days when cost-counting features largely in both business and personal situations, is the fact that a letter, whether sent somewhere in the United Kingdom at either first class or second class rate, or sent overseas, usually works out considerably cheaper to send than the most disciplined and short-lasting of telephone calls. There is also the fact to be taken into consideration that very few of us are disciplined about the length of telephone calls, even in the case of business calls when we know the other person quite well.

Especially if you know the person at the end of the line, even in a business call, there are usually pleasantries to be exchanged as well as information to be imparted and exchanged. Such pleasantries can be expensive in the case of overseas calls at peak times.

Written forms of communication have other advantages. Of extreme importance, particularly in a business context, is the fact that if you take the trouble to write you will have a permanent record of what you said—in the case of business letters it is always wise to keep a copy of letters you send. In addition, this allows you to absorb the contents of the reply at your leisure and compare it with your original letter. It also means that you can use either of the letters in evidence in the case of any dispute.

If you commit something to paper and the person who receives your letter telephones you in reply, it is always best to ask for the reply to be put in writing if there is the slightest possibility of any controversy arising in connection with the matter. This could be of relevance if you have made a written complaint about something and received a favourable telephone response from someone who later denies it. The alternative is to tape all such telephone calls, but this may seem rather extreme, except in cases of great importance.

The written form of communication has a further advantage over the spoken word. Because it is a permanent record that can come back to haunt them, people tend to take considerably more trouble about selecting, checking and organizing the information that they commit to paper than they do over information imparted over the telephone. Also, people writing a letter are faced visually with the results of their handiwork and for that reason are also more likely to put more effort into letters than they do into telephone calls.

Modern technology, to some extent, has enabled written forms of communication to retrieve the ground they had lost to the telephone. The introduction of fax machines has meant that people can enjoy some of the advantages of the telephone while still having the time to write the information that they wish to convey. A fax, therefore, can have the immediacy of the telephone but also some of the permanence of the letter. I say 'some of' because the paper that faxes are written on is rather flimsy and more easily torn or destroyed than the paper on which the average letter is written. People wishing to preserve the information on a fax would do well to copy it on to paper that is more substantial or consider investing in one of the newer fax machines that produce faxes on standard paper.

Theoretically, in common with the telephone, faxes should always get to the person to whom they are directed. I, however, have been unlucky on several occasions when I have tried to send a fax to someone who works for a relatively large organization. From time to time I have found that it has been accepted by the machinery at the other end but has never reached the person for whom it was intended, despite the identity of the intended recipient being made abundantly clear on the fax document. This may well be more of a comment on the organization concerned than on the fax system, but it is becoming a common problem in large, busy offices.

Lack of confidentiality can be a problem with the fax system. This may not be the case if you have your own fax system, but if you are an employee of a large organization it can cause embarrassment, whether the confidential fax is of a business or personal nature. The basic message is: if you do not want to share your business with your colleagues, avoid the fax machine.

Faxes have some other disadvantages. Fax is a shortened version of the word 'facsimile', the system on which it is based being known as 'facsimile transmission'. Such a system is based on the sending of the printed text and images through a telephone or other communication link. The document containing the printed text or image that is to be faxed is scanned and converted into digital code by a fax machine at the sending end and then transmitted to the fax machine at the receiving end. This machine then reconstitutes the received information into a printed copy of the original. Very often the information comes out as crystal clear at the receiving end as it went in at the sending end, but this is not always the case.

For various reasons—perhaps a gremlin in the system—faxes do not always arrive at the receiving end in such immaculate condition as to be instantly comprehensible. They are sometimes rather shadowy and difficult to make out, this being particularly true of cases in which maps, diagrams, tables, etc, are involved.

Faxes tend also to be expensive compared with the cost of a stamp and sometimes even with the cost of a quick, no-frills telephone call. Yet many people have abandoned all other forms of communication, irrespective of whether speed is really a concern, in favour of the fax. Indeed, I find that some people get quite upset if you have not got a fax machine, or access to a machine, and they find themselves having to send the requisite information by post.

There are those who argue that the fax system is to be welcomed because it has brought writing back into communication at a time when the telephone was beginning to reign supreme. This is true to some extent, but in general the art of letter-writing has not really been replaced by the fax. It is possible, for all I know, that there may be people somewhere out there who have made a fine art out of fax-writing and that even now they may be in the act of penning the most elegant of letters on a whole range of subjects—but I doubt it very much. I suppose that this may be a possibility for the future, but for the moment most people tend to use the most simple, short form of English, almost telegraphese in many cases, when preparing faxes.

This is because the fax started off life as a quick form of business communication. Nowadays, when more and more people have home computers and many have taken advantage of the potential to add a fax machine to the system, the fax is beginning to be used for more social forms of communication. At the moment, for the most part, these tend to be relatively short in length, of the nature of a quick note rather than a long newsy letter to a member of one's family.

The speed at which technology advances these days is truly mind-boggling. Before many people had grasped the concept of the fax, let alone begun to use it, the fax began to be replaced by electronic mail, otherwise known as e-mail or even email, a system by which messages are passed electronically from computer to computer.

Even before the fax machine became widespread, the telephone had had some of its power removed by the spread of the word processor. For some reason very few people in an office or other workplace, apart from secretaries employed for that very purpose, ever mastered the art of typing, or even tried to master it.

If people required a letter to be typed they had to write out what they wanted to say, hand this to a secretary, get it back again to check and sign, and get it back again corrected if there were any mistakes to be rectified. Alternatively, and of course this was particularly true of someone whose work included a great deal of correspondence, someone who might well have had a personal secretary, the content of letters was dictated to a secretary, taken down in shorthand by her—originally the majority of secretaries were women—and then typed and presented for checking and correcting.

As will be readily appreciated, all this took up a great deal of time and effort. Furthermore, it was clearly not a very satisfactory way of conveying information that was highly confidential or personal. But, curiously enough, not many non-secretarial staff in a firm thought of learning to type. Such an exercise was either regarded as being beneath their supposed intellectual ability and status or regarded as being too difficult.

Equally curiously, when the word processor became a standard piece of equipment in the office, and later in many homes, this attitude to typing seemed to change. Somehow, although doing one's own typing seemed lacking in prestige, this attitude was not transferred to the act of using a word processor—perhaps because of its new technology associations.

Also, many more people found that typing was not as difficult as they had assumed it to be. Admittedly they did not become competent touch typists overnight, but they could at least type relatively short documents using two or more fingers. It was also the case that the keyboard on the average word processor was easier to use by those who have never had typing lessons than that of the older style of typewriter. Perhaps most importantly, it was much easier to correct an error on a word processor than it was on an old style typewriter. Errors on documents typed by the latter process had to be eradicated by tell-tale correcting fluid, or else the whole letter had to be redone.

The result of this attitude brought about by word processors was that more people began to do their own typing. Of course, it is still unlikely that the head of a large corporation will be found tapping out his letters on his word processor or on the office computer, but certainly a much greater proportion of people in an office than ever before are to be found dealing with their own correspondence, reports and other forms of documentation. With a good deal of the effort having gone out of the process of letter-writing, and the removal of the necessity for an intermediary in the form of a secretary, some people even reverted to the written word at the expense of the telephone. The arrival of the fax machine, in combination with the word processor, increased the number of people turning their back on the telephone conversation, for business purposes at least.

This does not mean, however, that the wheel has gone full circle with reference to the letter and the telephone. Much of the material that goes out on the fax machine, as has been mentioned above, tends to take the form of telegraphese rather than flowing prose and so hardly merits the name of letter. Moreover, written communication can never be said to have retrieved the ground lost to spoken communication by means of the telephone until our social habits change. At the moment most of our social communication, if not conducted in person, is conducted by telephone.

To people of an older generation in particular this may seem a great pity, since they remember the joy of receiving long, newsy letters from friends and family and the joy of writing them. Alas pace of life and lack of time have conspired with the telephone against the writing of letters. This, in any event, is what we claim, although there are few of us who could not spare the time to write a letter if we really put our minds to it.

Of course, there are exceptions to this letterless environment. People with family members in the armed forces, or people with friends and family who live abroad, may well communicate by letter because of the difficulty or cost of telephoning, although this communication may often only take the form of a Christmas letter. Then we must not forget the fact that there are still people around, however few, who write letters rather than use the telephone for the very joy of writing them. However, for most of us, for most of the time, the pen is far from being mightier than the phone.

This is extremely unfortunate, not least because we have witnessed the demise of what once was, quite literally, an art form. Some early novels, such as *Pamela* (1749) by Samuel Richardson, were written in the form of letters and were thus known as epistolary novels. Also, some poetry took the form of epistolary verses, a notable example being 'An Epistle to Dr Arbuthnot' (1735) by Alexander Pope. Some of the material in the New Testament of the Bible is also in the form of letters, such as the Epistles of St Paul.

In a less literal way, letter-writing was an art form in the respect that many people wrote quite regularly and took a great deal of time and effort over what they had to say. Not only were there no telephones, but travel was far from easy, even over what would now be regarded as relatively short distances, and so letters were really substitutes for regular conversations between friends or between family members. Friends might well vie to outdo each other in witty written exchanges since they rarely got the opportunity to do so face to face.

However, prior to the invention of the prepaid penny postal system by Rowland Hill in 1840 and the establishment of a railway network, the exchange of letters was not an easy or cheap process. In those days, in order to send a letter one had to have the means to hire a private messenger. The person delivering the letter had to receive payment on delivery, the cost of delivery usually being related to the distance over which the letter had travelled. From the early sixteenth century the post-horse system, which gave its name to the modern post, replaced the personal messenger. This was a kind of relay system in which a series of horsemen were stationed at appointed places along the roads, waiting to take the mail to the next stage, or post, and the next horseman.

Another invention that eased the lot of the letter-writer, and thus undoubtedly encouraged more people to write, was that of the modern fountain pen by Lewis Edson Waterman around 1883. Waterman's fountain pen perfected earlier fountain pens, so called from having a reservoir of ink attached, by adding a device that slowed down the rate at which the ink got to the nib and thus stopped the pen leaking. Writing with this must certainly have been much less of a messy business than the quill pen and inkpot technique and must have required much less skill.

Requiring even less skill was the use of the Biro pen. This was called after the Hungarian-born Laszlo Biro, who patented the design in 1943. The principal feature of the Biro was that it had a ballpoint rather than a nib. It also employed quick-drying ink, which further reduced the possibility of leaking ink. This was the forerunner of all other ballpoint pens, now generally called biros, although Biro is a registered trademark.

The art of letter writing, then, despite its relatively recent fall from favour, has enjoyed several surges in popularity through the ages. Today, the decrease in letter-writing, particularly in social letters, has deprived both the family historian and the social historian of a valuable source of information, since the content of letters might well have represented an informal record of what was going on at the time of writing both in the family and in wider society. Many people seeking to find out more about their ancestors, at least about their more recent ones, have found family letters extremely useful and historians have found that informal letters are often helpful in throwing light on the social conditions that prevailed at a particular time.

Others who are likely to have cause to regret the demise of the social letter are biographers. Personal letters, both from and to their subjects, have given biographers an extremely valuable insight into character, temperament, relationships and circumstances. The reduction in letter-writing has deprived them of a potential treasure trove.

We should not wallow in too much emotion at the seeming demise of the letter. Letter-writing has undoubtedly fallen from its former glory, but it is far from dead. It certainly retains enough life for it to be worthwhile for people to learn the techniques of it, even if one day these techniques are used solely in the context of faxes or e-mail.

Chapter 2

General Advice

As has been indicated in the previous chapter, letter-writing generally requires more time and effort than using the telephone. It also tends to require more in the way of decision-making—a process that starts even before you have set pen to paper.

It could be said that if you write a letter you are either trying to make a good impression on someone or at least trying to indicate to someone that you are a person of account who is not to be taken lightly. If this was not the case you would probably just have lifted the phone.

Writing paper
With this in mind, it is important to give some thought to the question of paper. If it is your intention to put over a favourable impression of yourself it is clearly not a good idea simply to tear a piece of paper from one of your child's school exercise books and start writing. This is going to look both scrappy and sloppy—and will be treated as such.

Since the letter is likely to be of importance in some area of your life it is worth investing in good quality writing paper that is not too thin and flimsy. Not only does the latter tear easily but it looks cheap and nasty and gets you off to a bad start with the recipient of your communication. The use of such paper is all very well in a long newsy airmail letter to a friend overseas if you are particularly hard-up, and even then only if you have exceptionally legible handwriting, but should otherwise be avoided.

When choosing writing paper it is important to opt for the plain and simple. Avoid coloured paper, especially when the colour is of rather a strident nature, unless the letter that you intend writing is of a personal nature and you are absolutely certain that the intended recipient is a devotee of violet, peach or turquoise, or whatever colour paper you have selected. Pale cream, pale blue or pale grey may look tasteful and may be all very well as the basis for social letters, but for purposes of formal business letters it is best to stick to white.

It should go without saying that anything in the way of fancy illustration should not appear on writing paper on which a business letter or reasonably formal personal letter is to be written. Writing paper with roses, birds, teddy bears, etc, cavorting around its edges should be kept strictly for close friends who like this kind of paper and who use it themselves.

If you are thinking of having your address and telephone number pre-printed or engraved on your personal writing paper it is again important to avoid anything too fancy and instead to opt for something that is simple and understated. Something that looks as though it ought to be lit up by neon lighting is not a good idea if you want to make a serious impression. If, of course, you are writing on your firm's writing paper you have no choice in the matter and in any case people tend to be less censorious of business writing paper than they are of personal writing paper. Should you be starting up your own business, and are not of an artistic turn of mind it is worth consulting a reliable designer to help you select something that is eye-catching but not overwhelming and that is appropriate to the nature of your business.

Also to be avoided is lined paper, even if your handwriting is of the kind that slopes ever more upwards or ever more downwards with every word you write. However unjust it may seem to you, lined paper has an uneducated look about it, perhaps because it carries memories of the schoolroom with it. If you find it difficult to write with any degree of straightness you could try using a ruled backing sheet under your unlined paper, provided you make sure that it does not slip. Should you reject this suggestion you are just going to have to practise writing on unlined paper until you get it right—and straight.

The size of writing paper should also be given some thought. If the letter that you are going to write is to be directed at a firm or organization you may well decide to use a size of paper known as A4. This is a standard size in business (29.7 x 21 cm, 11³/4 x 8¹/4 in) and will fit into a filing system. Should you not have very much to say you should be careful how you lay out the letter—*see* Chapter Three on Presentation and Layout.

If the letter is not directed at a firm there is no requirement to use A4. You should still give some thought, however, to the amount that you think you are likely to write and the nature of your handwriting when you are deciding on size of writing paper. Should you be planning to write a very long newsy letter to a friend and your handwriting is of the large, sprawling variety, then it is clearly sensible to choose a large page size—otherwise you are going to end up with a small but very fat bundle of paper to post. On the other hand, if you are writing rather a formal personal letter and you know that you have very little to say—you may, for example, be thanking a distant cousin for a present that you did not really want—it would be best to opt for a much smaller page size, especially if you have very small, rather cramped handwriting. A few lines on a sea of paper will simply draw attention to the fact that you had very little to say

It is best to avoid notelets, especially those of a highly colourful or fancy nature, unless you are writing to a very close friend or a member of your family. They are not appropriate in a formal letter as they create a very informal impression, and a communication written on a colourful notelet is much less likely to be taken seriously than one written on plain paper.

Nowadays there is less objection to writing on both sides of a piece of writing paper than there used to be, in the case of personal letters at least, and it certainly saves paper in these conservation-conscious days. In the case of business letters it is best not to economize on paper by writing or typing on both sides of it.

Before you send a letter with writing on both sides of the paper to anyone, be sure that both sides are actually legible. If the paper is thin and the writer has pressed very heavily with a pen with a thick nib or point and dark ink, the writing may be very difficult to read. It is unfair to send such a letter to your correspondent, who may have to spend hours trying to decipher what is written and who may in despair or frustration in the end throw the communication out unread.

Envelopes
When it comes to choosing an envelope for your communication it is best to select a good quality, fairly substantial one that matches your writing paper—unless the communication is quite bulky, in which case you should find an envelope to fit it, often pale brown in colour. Thus, if you have chosen to ignore the advice to go for white or plain in your choice of writing paper and gone for paper of a bright purple colour, you should stick with your choice and go for a bright purple colour of envelope and hope that it does not dazzle the postman.

If the letter is a business communication or a fairly formal letter, especially to someone whose tastes you do not know, it is important to avoid decorated envelopes. Some business letters are routinely sent in brown envelopes, supposedly because it is less easy to detect an enclosure in a brown envelope than it is in a white one, although this to some extent depends on the thickness of the envelope. In the past, small brown envelopes were used for sending out bills and most of us were not too keen on receiving such communications. However, this practice is not so widespread now, and many bills today come through the letterbox in plain white envelopes.

When choosing an envelope, care should be taken to select one that is large enough to hold your letter easily. Letters should be folded as little as possible, both in the inter-

ests of legibility and in the interests of creating a good
impression. Do not scrunch a large letter up until it fits a
small envelope. For larger communications, or for letters
written on fairly large sheets of paper that you do not wish
to fold, there is a wide range of envelopes available, often
pale brown in colour.

Cards

Those who do not really like writing letters, or who find
them difficult to write, are often tempted to send a card instead since these require less effort to write. Greetings
cards, however, do require effort in selecting a card that is
suitable to the occasion and to the taste of the sender and
intended recipient. This can be a lengthy business, although there now seem to be more relatively plain cards
around with either a simple message or no message at all,
and an attractive, or at least inoffensive, picture on the
front, a welcome change for many of us from the flowery
verses that used to be the norm.

There are many occasions on which greetings cards are
perfectly acceptable, whether you choose to send a card
designed specifically for the occasion or a 'no-message'
one on which you write your own greeting. If a close
friend or family member passes a driving test or graduates
from university it is quite appropriate to send a card
rather than write a letter. Likewise, if someone is ill it is
appropriate to send a card. Often, people in such circumstances appreciate a little humour.

Some occasions, on the other hand, are rather more
tricky since whether to send a card or not depends on the
likely reaction of the recipient. If you have been a guest in

someone's house, for example, and wish to thank your host and hostess, it may seem tempting to send a quick card, whether this takes the form of a greetings card or postcard, but the said host or hostess, especially if they are of an older generation, may be sticklers for formality and expect a letter, the kind of letter that used to be called a 'bread and butter letter', thanking them for their hospitality and saying a few words about how pleasant your stay with them was.

I myself avoid sending 'sympathy' cards on the occasion of a bereavement. If you are moved enough by the death of someone to wish to send some form of communication to the bereaved, it is worth writing a letter trying to indicate how you feel. Sending a card can give the impression that you are just going through the motions of sympathy without trying to express it, even if this is not actually the case.

Postcards, as opposed to greetings cards that are placed in an envelope, have the disadvantage of being easily read by anyone who comes into contact with them. If you wish to avoid this you can always put the postcard into an envelope, but this destroys one of their greatest advantages, the fact that having written it you can put it straight into the postbox without having to bother with an envelope.

There are several occasions when postcards are quite appropriate, although, as is the case with greetings cards, they should not be sent to people who might feel offended by such a brief form of communication instead of a letter. Postcards, for example, are ideal if you are moving house and wish to advise others of your change of address. They are also useful for sending information about an appointment and so on, information that is of a non-personal nature and suitable for the eyes of the world, and are often mandatory when entering some forms of competition. Some people find it worthwhile to have some postcards pre-printed with their address and phone number, and sometimes name, for use on appropriate occasions.

The above information refers mainly to plain postcards but, of course, many postcards have a picture on one side and are therefore known, not surprisingly, as picture postcards. They are used frequently by people who are on holiday or on a day trip somewhere. On such occasions their use is absolutely standard and part of convention. No one has any right to object to receiving a picture postcard card with a brief standard message instead of a long letter from someone who is on holiday. Everyone should accept that holidays are for giving the brain, as well as the body, a rest.

Writing tools

So much for the material on which you write your letter. Now for what you write it with. If you decide to write a letter rather than type it or have it typed, it is important to choose a pen that will make your handwriting as legible and as neat and attractive-looking as possible, particularly if you wish to make a good impression on someone. For example, my handwriting, which is regrettably practically illegible, especially if I am writing quickly, looks better if I write with a pen with a very narrow nib or point. Other people may find that a fairly broad nib is more suited to their writing.

There has been a marked increase in recent years in the

use of fountain pens as many people feel that their handwriting is at its best when they use one. Certainly it can be more of a pleasure to write with a fountain pen, and handwriting penned by one does tend to look better. There are very handsome fountain pens around, some of them quite expensive, and there are people who feel that it adds in some way to their status to write with a good-quality fountain pen. If, however, you are like me and are continually losing pens, the fountain pen may not be an economical possibility. I lose so many pens that I would spend a fortune replacing them in no time.

The ballpoint pen, or biro, is considerably cheaper than a good-quality fountain pen and on the whole is easier and quicker to use. One of its early advantages over the fountain pen was that it was less likely to leak. Unfortunately, it is by no means unknown for a ballpoint pen to leak, particularly one of a cheaper variety. The linings of several of my handbags can testify to this. A letter written with a leaky ballpoint will be blotchy and messy, as well as being difficult to read, and creates a bad impression. There are some very good ones around, which are still relatively inexpensive, and it is worth investing in one if the letter that you intend writing is important to you.

It is also worth giving some thought to ink colour. The best approach is to stick to either blue or black ink, whichever you prefer, as they are the most unobtrusive and the most generally acceptable. Coloured inks, such as red or green, are all very well if you are writing a very informal letter to a close friend but should be avoided in more formal letters. Certain people, such as teachers, who routinely use pens with coloured ink in the course of their work, often find that they cannot lay their hands on a black or blue pen and frequently use a coloured ink pen to sign cheques or perform other essential acts of writing.

To write or type?
Deciding whether to type or write a letter never used to trouble most people because they were either unable to type or did not have access to a typewriter. Nowadays, the decision presents a very real problem since more people now type and have home typewriters, and even more have home word processors or computers and can make a fair attempt at typing or keyboarding.

Two things in particular should be taken into consideration. One is the likely reaction and attitude of your intended recipient. Some will prefer the typed communication to the handwritten and verse versa. It is difficult to please everyone but it is worth trying to.

The recipient of a business letter will almost certainly prefer to receive a typed communication. It is standard practice in business, and most business people have neither the time nor the inclination to spend time deciphering a handwritten letter. Indeed, handwritten business letters, because of the extra time and effort they involve and because they generally create a less professional image, are likely to receive less serious attention than a typed one. Thus, it is better if you can possibly arrange it to type your business communications—word processor keyboards are easier to operate than you might think. Indeed, if it is of particular importance, for example a letter to a lawyer, and you cannot type it yourself, it may well be worthwhile getting someone to type it for you.

It should be noted in passing that it is wise, and often essential, to keep a copy of any business correspondence that you send. In this respect the word processor has been a great boon since you can print off as many copies of a communication as you wish and keep it on floppy disk for future reference. Word processors also give one the facility to correct errors electronically and thus save you from either having to type the whole thing over again or use correcting fluid, as was formerly the case.

A fairly recent development in business communication is the practice of some firms to ask applicants for jobs to send in letters of application in their own handwriting. Before the boom in typing and word processing, most applicants would automatically have applied for jobs by means of a handwritten letter. Nowadays, however, unless otherwise instructed many applicants would type a letter of application or have it typed for them with a view to sending as professional looking an application as possible. So why do some firms seem to be turning the clock back? There may be some jobs where legibility of handwriting still matters, and there may be some firms that feel that the neatness or otherwise of the handwriting may give a clue to the applicant's likely approach to the job.

There is also an increasing tendency for some firms, particularly large firms, to have letters handwritten by applicants scrutinized by trained graphologists. By this technique they hope to get an insight into the applicant's character, personality and suitability for the job. Recruiting new staff is a time-consuming and costly business and appointing the wrong person to the job is even more costly. With the help of graphologists some firms hope to avoid this.

Where personal letters are concerned you must once again think of the likely reaction of the recipient. Despite the increase in the number of people who can type or keyboard there is a feeling around, especially among older people, that a handwritten letter is more personal and more caring. Thus, it is probably best to write your personal letters rather than type them, unless you are absolutely certain that the other person has no objection to a typed communication.

However, there is a second point to be taken into consideration when making the choice between writing and typing. It is quite simply the legibility or otherwise of your handwriting. Most of us tend to be rather optimistic about the legibility of our handwriting, although I personally am an exception to this tendency, since so many people over the years have pointed out the sheer illegibility of mine. Indeed,if I have written something in a hurry I cannot read it myself.

People with handwriting that is difficult, not to say impossible, to read should type even personal letters unless this will really give undue offence. The alternative is for the recipient to spend long periods of time trying to decipher the scribble and making intelligent guesses at the contents. The latter exercise can be quite fun if you have the time. I have one friend who writes or types an airmail letter to me about once a year. Her typed versions are gone in a few minutes, but her handwritten versions can take several days—on and off at snatched moments—and a good deal of guesswork.

Typed and handwritten versions contain about the same amount of news and yet I feel that I have got more out of the handwritten version and that I have more time with her, which of course I have.

In situations where it does not really matter whether you write or type, it is worth taking into consideration the fact that if you make a mistake in a handwritten letter you either have to start again and rewrite the whole letter or score out individual words and rewrite them, which looks messy and careless. Word processors, as has been mentioned above, and some modern electronic typewriters allow one to correct errors electronically and so the offending mistakes are never revealed in print.

However difficult your handwriting is to decipher, there are occasions when you must try particularly hard to write neatly and when the recipient must use a little tolerance and a great deal of ingenuity in the art of deciphering. Letters of condolence to the bereaved, love letters, and other letters of a particularly personal nature should be handwritten, however illegible your handwriting.

I have a personal dislike of supposedly personal letters that are typed but have the initial greeting (e.g. 'Dear Mary') and the closing greeting (e.g. 'Yours sincerely, John) in handwriting. This practice is widely held to personalize the seemingly impersonal nature of the typed letter, but I always have the sneaking feeling that it looks like an afterthought or like an attempt to deceive you into thinking that the letter is more personal than it actually is —that it has not gone out to several others, rather along the lines of the typed Christmas letter that some people

send out either with or without a Christmas card to keep
you up-to-date with the doings of the various members of
their family. This attempt at personalization is not re-
stricted to typed personal letters. It is also found in business letters to give them rather a spurious suggestion of
friendliness and is particularly common in letters asking
for donations to a charity or other organization.

Summary

If you are going to take the trouble to write a letter you
should aim for as professional a final product as possible.
In order to do so, it is worthwhile spending some time and
thought on choosing the best paper and writing instrument
that you can afford. This will help you to create a good
impression on the recipient of your letter. There are other
issues that also help to do these and they are described in
the following chapters.

Chapter 3

Presentation and Layout

Finding the motivation to begin is often the most difficult part of letter-writing. It is all too easy to keep putting off the task, sometimes until it is too late.

When you have summoned up the necessary motivation there is the question of layout to be considered first. If the letter is going to create a favourable impression presentation is all-important. You do not wish to give the impression that you have just thrown the letter together hastily and carelessly.

Address of the sender

There are certain conventions to be observed when considering the layout of a letter. One of these concerns the address of the sender. This, including the postcode, should be placed in the top right -hand corner of the sheet of paper. Formerly it was standard practice to indent each line of the address and this is still common today, as:

```
              23 Park Drive,
                Seafield,
                  Blackshire,
                    RA14 2TY
```

However, it is now becoming customary not to indent the lines of the sender's address but simply to have the first letter of the second line placed immediately under the first letter of the first line and so on, as:

```
        23 Park Drive,
        Seafield,
        Blackshire,
        RA14 2TY
```

It was formally the practice to place a comma at the end of each line of the address of the sender. Now, however, there is a general tendency to use less punctuation than was formerly the case, and it is now common to dispense with punctuation in addresses, whether or not they are indented, as:

```
        23 Park Drive
         Seafield
          Blackshire
           RA14 2TY
```

or

```
        23 Park Drive
        Seafield
        Blackshire
        RA14 2TY
```

Abbreviations in addresses

Abbreviations are common in some parts of addresses, although the full forms are also frequently used in some cases. When abbreviations are used, the question of whether or not to put a full stop arises. Abbreviations that are formed from the first and last letters of words and are in fact contractions should not be given full stops. Thus you would use *Rd* (or *Road*), *St* (or *Street*), *Mt* (or *Mount*), *Mr* (*Mister* is rarely used), and so on.

In the case of abbreviations that are not contractions but abbreviations that are simply the beginning letters of words, full stops were formerly required, as *ref.* for *reference*, and *Esq.* (*Esquire* is rarely used). Nowadays, however, there has been a general decline in the amount of punctuation used and such abbreviations are now frequently found without full stops, *ref* and *Esq*, for example.

The names of counties are frequently abbreviated in addresses, whether in the letter or on the envelope. Since these are not abbreviations that are contractions but abbreviations in the same category as *ref.* for *reference* described above, abbreviations of counties would formerly always have ended with a full stop, as *Lancs.* for *Lancashire*, but nowadays, following a general decrease in punctuation, they are frequently found without a full stop, as *Yorks* for *Yorkshire*.

Postcode

The postcode is often placed on a separate line after the county, as opposite. Alternatively, it can be placed on the same line as the county, although this sometimes makes for rather a long line, and is discouraged by the post office.

Telephone number

Some people choose to put their telephone number on letters, and certainly it can often be useful to the recipient of a letter, if not entirely necessary. The positioning of a telephone number, and, if appropriate, the fax number, is to some extent a matter of taste. The telephone number can be placed under the postcode, usually leaving a blank line between the postcode and the telephone number, in line with the first line of the address where this has been indented, as:

```
                    23 Park Drive,
                      Seafield,
                       Blackshire,
                        RA14 2TY

               Tel: 01X1 222444
```

Since the date also has to be placed somewhere with the address, the right-hand corner of your sheet of paper can become quite crowded, and some people choose to place the telephone number somewhere at the top of the left-hand side of the paper. It is sometimes positioned on the same line as the first line of the address, as:

```
   Tel: 01X1 222444              23 Park Drive,
                                   Seafield,
                                    Blackshire,
                                     RA14 2TY
```

Alternatively, the telephone number can be placed on the same line as another line of the address, often that of the postcode, as:

```
                                    23 Park Drive,
                                    Seafield,
                                    Blackshire,
        Tel: 01X1 222444            RA14 2TY
```

Pre-printed letterheads
Some people choose to take some of the trouble out of the layout of letters by having their addresses pre-printed on their writing paper. Of course this is standard practice on business stationery and the majority of larger companies spend quite a lot of time, effort and money on acquiring an eye-catching design that will reflect what they wish to project as their corporate image. It will normally include their name, address, telephone number and fax number, often along the top of the page. However, many private individuals now have pre-printed letterheads for both personal and business stationery. In the case of personal stationery, some people choose to have their pre-printed letterhead centred at the top of the page instead of having it in the more traditional place at the top right-hand corner of the page. Others choose to have their telephone number included, but others choose simply to have their addresses printed and to write their telephone numbers on those letters that they wish to carry it.

Date

The date should be placed under the postcode. There is often a line left blank between the postcode and the date. In cases where the lines of the address are indented the date is usually aligned with the first line of the address, as:

```
              23 Park Drive,
                 Seafield,
                  Blackshire,
                   RA14 2TY.


              24 May 1996
```

Various forms of the date are possible. Some people opt for the style given above, i.e. *24 May 1996* but some prefer to use *24th May 1996*. Others again adopt the style that is more common in North America, i.e. *May 24, 1996*. Putting the date in numbers only is also a possibility, i.e. *24/5/96* or *24:5:96,* but indicating the month by name makes for speed of reference, especially when back correspondence is being consulted. Also, people who prefer to use numbers in dates should be aware that in North America the month is placed first, rather than the day of the month. Thus *24 May 1996* would be *5/24/96*.

Address of recipient

If you are writing a personal letter there is no need to include the address of the person to whom the letter is being sent, but if you are sending a business letter you should include this. It should be placed on the left-hand side of the sheet of paper starting on the line after the date—sometimes a blank line is left between the date and the start of the address of the intended recipient. Unlike the address of the sender, the address of the person to whom the letter is being sent is not usually indented. If the name of the person to whom your business letter is addressed is known to you, this should be included as well, as:

```
Tel: 01X1 222444              23 Park Drive,
                                 Seafield,
                                   Blackshire,
                                     RA14 2TY


                              24 May 1966


Mr James Black
The Manager,
Cosmo Furniture Store,
12-15 King Street,
Seafield,
Blackshire,
RA11 6DR
```

Often in a business communication the date is put at the right-hand corner, not immediately under the address of the sender, but aligned with the postcode of the address of the intended recipient, as:

```
Tel: 01X1 222444              23 Park Drive,
                                Seafield,
                                  Blackshire,
                                    RA14 2TY


Mr James Black
The Manager,
Cosmo Furniture Store,
12-15 King Street,
Seafield,
Blackshire,
RA11 6DR                      24 May 1966
```

Formerly it was fairly common to use the abbreviation *Esq* or *Esq.* after a man's name with a comma before it instead of *Mr* before the name, as *James Black, Esq,* but this is fairly uncommon nowadays and is considered rather formal. Nowadays it is also quite usual to omit the *Mr* but not to add *Esq*. Only the name is used, as *James Black,* but this is considered by some people to be a little informal.

If a first name is reduced to an initial this was formerly always followed by a full stop, as *Mr J. Black* or *J. A. Black, Esq*. It is best to follow this convention but nowadays it is quite common to find initials without full stops as the general level of punctuation has decreased.

Companies in addresses
The name of some companies is followed by *Ltd*, indicating that they are limited companies. Others are followed

by *plc* or *PLC*, indicating that they are public limited
companies, as:

```
The Manager,
The World Book Company plc,
43 Potter Row,
London,
W1P 6DKW


The Managing Director,
Smithfield Properties Ltd,
34 Station Road,
Birchingham,
B2P 6RPJ
```

Reference numbers

If you are replying to a business letter you should quote
any reference number that is on it as this will speed up
the process of dealing with the contents of your letter.
If you have a reference you should also include it, although this is less likely if you are a private individual
who is writing a business letter rather than an employee
of a firm writing on its behalf.

The word 'reference' is usually abbreviated and formerly was always spelt with a full stop, although the full
stop is now frequently omitted. The reference number is
usually placed under the date and on the same line as the
first line of the recipient's address, as:

```
Tel: 01X1 222444              23 Park Drive,
                                Seafield,
                                  Blackshire,
                                    RA14 2TY


The Manager                   Ref. JM/Dk19
Cosmo Furniture Store,
12-15 King Street,
Seafield,
Blackshire,
RA11 6DR                      24 May 1966
```

Opening greeting

The opening greeting should begin at the edge of the page and be placed under the last line of the recipient's address, where this has been included, often with a line left blank, as:

```
The Manager,
Cosmo Furniture Store,
12-15 King Street,
Seafield,
RA11 6DR.


Dear Sir,
```

In the case of personal letters where there is no recipient's address the opening greeting should go at the left-hand side after the date, usually with a line left blank, as:

```
                              23 Park Drive,
                              Seafield,
                              Blackshire,
                              RA14 2TY.


                              24 May 1966

  Dear Mary,
```

How you address the intended recipient of your letter in your opening greeting depends on who the person is and on your relationship to the person. If you know it is a man to whom you are writing but you do not know his name, it is still standard practice to write *Dear Sir*. This sounds very formal in these rather informal days and there are people who are in favour of using the title or job of the person addressed in your opening greeting, as:

```
  Dear Manager,

  Dear Personnel Officer,
```

If you are comfortable with this form of address and you are confident that the person to whom you are writing will find it perfectly acceptable then that is fine. Of course the problem is that you might not be in a position to know that such a greeting will be acceptable to the intended recipient of your letter and it might well not be.

This approach does at least have the advantage that a greeting that denotes the job of the recipient of your letter is likely to be unisex. This gets around the problem of not knowing whether the person to whom your letter is addressed is a man or a woman.

If you know that the person to whom your letter is addressed is a woman and do not know her name, then the standard conventional greeting is *Dear Madam*. This sounds even more formal than *Dear Sir*, but at the moment the only way around this is to adopt the style mentioned above of greeting the person in terms of the person's job.

The situation is even worse if you do not know the sex of the person to whom you are writing. The conventional standard letter greeting in such a situation is *Dear Sir or Madam*, which sounds extremely formal indeed. It is in this situation that even *Dear Manager*, for example, might seem more acceptable to some, but I have not got to that stage yet. For the moment at least I am sticking with *Dear Sir or Madam*, however unsatisfactory this may be.

If you are writing to a firm and you know very little about the set-up, it is still quite common practice to use the opening greeting *Dear Sirs*. This is used formally if you are writing to more than one man, as to the partners in a firm, without specifying who they are. *Messrs.* can also be used if you are writing to more than one man by name. This was formerly quite common but is now considered a bit old-fashioned. However, it is still used, particularly in business letters, as:

```
Dear Messrs. Brown, Green and Black,
```

Even if you do know the name of the person to whom you are writing, your problems are not over. Not so long ago there would have been no problem. You would either have been on first name terms with someone or you would not have been. Friends and family members were addressed at the beginning of a letter by their first names, such as *Dear James* or *Dear Jane* or by their relationship to you, as *Dear Mother* or *Dear Father*. Business correspondents who were known to you were addressed in such terms as *Dear Mr Brown* or *Dear Miss James*.

Nowadays things have changed a bit. If you know someone's name but do not know him or her well enough to use just a first name you can opt for such letter greetings as *Dear Peter Smith* or *Dear Anne Jones*, this being considered less formal than *Dear Mr Smith* or *Dear Miss Jones* and a kind of halfway house between these and the familiar *Dear Peter* or *Dear Anne*. It is a convention that was much disliked by several people at first but is now becoming widespread.

This new convention gets around the problem of how to address women, whether to call them *Miss*, *Mrs* or *Ms*, it being very difficult to establish the marital status of all the women to whom one might write. *Ms*, which can refer to all women, removes the need to know whether a woman is married or not. When first introduced there was a great deal of opposition to it as it was felt to be very ugly, but it has now been generally accepted, if not necessarily welcomed.

It is sometimes difficult to decide how to address certain people. These include people with titles and people who occupy a particular position in public life. Some information is given on this in Appendix A.

Closing greeting

This is placed under the last paragraph—there is often a blank line between the two—and above the signature. Some choice is possible as to the positioning of the closing greeting. There are some people who prefer to place it towards the right, as:

```
I hope that you will attend to this matter
as soon as possible.
                        Yours sincerely,
```

Others prefer to place the closing greeting towards the left, as:

```
I hope that you will attend to this matter
as soon as possible.

Yours sincerely,
```

Others again prefer to place the closing greeting in the centre, as;

```
I hope that you will attend to this matter
as soon as possible.

            Yours sincerely,
```

The closing greeting can take various forms. It was formerly the strict convention that letters that began with the opening greeting *Dear Sir* or *Dear Madam* should end with the closing greeting *Yours faithfully*. Many people still adhere to this convention but others feel that it is peculiar and inappropriate to bring the concept of faithfulness into a letter to someone whom one does not know, it not really being a situation where the concept of fidelity is relevant. On the whole it sounds rather stuffy in what is an age that is much less formal than previous ages.

People who dislike *Yours faithfully* or feel that it is inappropriate opt for *Yours sincerely*, even when they use the opening greeting *Dear Sir* or *Dear Madam*. Formerly this was used only when the opening greeting was more personal. Thus, if you began a letter *Dear Mr Jones* or *Dear Mrs Smith* you would close it with *Yours sincerely*. If it was even more personal and you began your letter with *Dear John* or *Dear Mary* you would still close it with *Yours sincerely*, unless the person was a close friend or relative, in which case you might opt for something more affectionate. The *Yours sincerely* convention still applies, except that its use has been extended in some cases to more formal letters.

If your correspondent is a close personal friend you might choose to close the letter with something even less formal than *Yours sincerely* such as *Yours affectionately*, *Yours ever*, or just *Yours*. The closing greetings *love* or *With Love* should be kept for those correspondents for whom you have a really deep affection and with whom you have a really close relationship, although nowadays many people use the greeting very lavishly and very loosely, particularly on postcards or greetings cards.

It is sometimes useful to put a closing greeting that is warmer than *Yours sincerely* but more formal and less affectionate than those suggested for close friends or relative. In such a situation *Best wishes* or *With all best wishes* is usually quite suitable.

Signature

As has been mentioned above, the signature is placed under the closing greeting, usually with a blank line between them. Since not everyone's signature is legible—indeed some people seem to pride themselves on the very illegibility of their signatures—it is important to place your name underneath your signature so that people are in no doubt about the identity of the writer of the letter and in no doubt about the exact name of the person to whom they should address a reply, as:

```
I hope that you will attend to this matter
as soon as possible.


Yours sincerely,


James Brown

James Brown
```

In business letters it is also a good idea to include your position in an organization or firm where this is relevant, as:

```
I hope that you will attend to this matter
as soon as possible.

Yours sincerely,
```

James Brown

```
James Brown
Club Secretary
```

Sometimes people sign letters on behalf of someone else. This is particularly common in the case of a secretary or assistant who signs a letter for a boss who has written a letter, or who is at least responsible for it, but is unable to sign it because of absence from the office, for example. This often appears as follows:

```
I hope that you will attend to this matter
as soon as possible.

Yours sincerely,
```

Jane Green

```
Jane Green
p.p. James Brown
```

However, *p.p.* does not stand for *on behalf of*, as is generally assumed, but is an abbreviation of the Latin phrase *per procurationem*, meaning *by proxy*. Thus, *p.p.* should really precede the name of the person signing the letter rather than the name of the person on whose behalf the letter is being signed, but modern practice does not follow this.

The practice of getting someone else to sign one's letters is a practice disliked by many people, and they are offended when they receive one, particularly if it is not a circular. The theory behind the practice is that letters might get unduly delayed if the person who had written was going to be out of the office for some time. There is no doubt, however, that it is quite common for people almost automatically to get their secretaries to sign their outgoing mail if they are busy or if they simply cannot be bothered.

It is important to remember to sign your letters. If you are in a hurry it is all to easy to type a letter on the word processor, print it out and put it in an envelope without signing it. Since you will have typed your name on it there will be no problem for the recipient in identifying the sender, but unsigned letters can cause offence.

Addressing envelopes

When you are addressing envelopes you should ideally start writing about halfway down the envelope but legibilty is the most important thing about addressing an envelope. If Post Office staff cannot read the address it will not be delivered, and if they have extreme difficulty in making it out there may well be a delay in the delivery

of the letter. Should you have handwriting that is known
to be difficult to read you could try printing the address if
it is not possible to type it or have it typed.

The conventions relating to addressing envelopes are
similar to those relating to writing addresses in letters.
The person's name goes on the first line and the address
follows. The house number, not forgetting flat number
where relevant, and street comes first in the address, followed by the town, county and postcode. The postcode
does not always have a line to itself but sometimes this is
necessary for reasons of space or clarity.

As is the case with addresses in letters, the address on
envelopes is frequently indented, as:

```
        Mr James Brown,
          Flat 3,
            23 Whitehill Street,
              Seafield,
                Blackshire,
                  RA9 5JX
```

However, it is now common for the lines of the address
to be placed one under the other with no indentation, as:

```
        Mr James Brown,
        Flat 3,
        23 Whitehill Street,
        Seafield,
        Blackshire,
        RA9 5JX
```

As is the case with addresses in letters, there is often minimal punctuation on envelope addresses nowadays, as:

```
Mr James Brown
Flat 3
23 Whitehill Street
Seafield
Blackshire
RA9 5JX
```

Some people choose to print addresses in block capital letters for clarity. Others write most of the address in ordinary handwriting but print the town in block capital letters, especially if this is a large town to make it more prominent, a feature appreciated by those involved in the postal service, as:

```
Mr James Brown
Flat 3
23 Whitehill Street
SEAFIELD
Blackshire
RA9 5JX
```

Further information is given earlier in this chapter on addresses in letters, whether these addresses are of senders or of intended recipients, and much of this information is also relevant to addresses on envelopes. See in particular the section dealing with abbreviations in addresses.

Main text

Much of the information relating to the main text of the letter will relate either to the actual content or to the language and style, which is dealt with in the next chapter, but there are some features of it that are connected with how the letter looks, and so should be dealt with under presentation.

Headings

If you are writing a business letter, and particularly if there is likely to be a series of letters on a specific subject, it is useful to put a heading at the top of your letter so that your recipient can see immediately what the letter is about. If such a heading is used it should be underlined and be placed after the opening greeting, often with a line left blank between them. The heading can be centred or placed at the left-hand side according to choice and according to the layout of the rest of the letter. For example if you intend placing your closing greeting at the left-hand side you might also decide to place the heading of the letter at the left-hand side, as:

```
Dear Mr Hunt,


Repairs to 24 Seaview Terrace
```

If you intend placing your closing greeting either in the centre or at the right-hand side of the page then you might well choose to position the heading in the centre of the page, particularly if you have indented the paragraphs (see below). The first paragraph begins immediately after the heading, often with a blank line between the heading and opening paragraph, as:

```
Dear Mr Smith,


          Repairs to 24 Seaview Terrace


I am once again writing to draw your
attention to the fact that the repairs to
my garage undertaken by your firm are still
not complete.
```

Paragraphs

Information on paragraphs is given in the next chapter on style and language. However, paragraphs must also be mentioned in respect to the layout and presentation of letters.

Formerly it was the standard convention to indent the start of each new paragraph, including the first one after the opening greeting, as:

```
Dear Mr Porter,
    I enclose a cheque for £200, being the
amount of rent due for the month of February.
    Unfortunately I shall be leaving the city
soon and will have to give up the flat at 52
Queen Street. I am thus giving you two
months' notice as from today.
```

Nowadays it is very common for paragraphs not to be indented. This also applies to the opening paragraph, as:

```
Dear Mary,

Thank you very much for the generous book
token that you sent for my birthday. I have
already exchanged it for a copy of the new
biography of Dickens.

I hope that you will be able to come and
visit us in the summer. June would be the
best month for us but let us know what
suits you.
```

Summary
These then are some of the conventions relating to the layout and presentation of letters and envelopes. As you will have seen, there is some scope for choice in some cases, such as in the positioning of telephone and reference numbers. In addition, the general layout of a letter must be decided according to the size of the paper that you use and according to the length of your letter.

Chapter 4

The Nuts and Bolts
of Letter Writing

Obviously what you say in your letter is of supreme importance but how you say it is also important. If the letter is not articulate and well constructed it may be far from clear what point you are actually trying to make. Should it prove a struggle to do so, your recipient will just give up in the attempt.

Just as it is vital to get the layout and presentation of your letter right if you are going to create a favourable impression on the person who receives it, so you must get the words, grammar and punctuation correct. There is nothing more annoying to some people than receiving an ill-spelt, ungrammatical letter. Just think, the person who receives your job application could be one of them.

How much effort you want to put into your letter will to a very large extent depend on what the purpose of the letter is and to whom you are sending it. If you are simply sending a gossipy letter to someone who has been your best friend from your schooldays there is no need to check your grammar and punctuation since she is going to be more interested in the content of your letter, particularly if the gossip is exceptionally juicy, and might not even notice any errors.

Others, however, may not take you seriously if they receive a letter that is full of errors. This is true not only of recipients of job applications but people who are on the receiving end of letters of complaint and a whole range of other people. A letter that is written in grammatical English that is correctly spelt and punctuated will give the impression of an educated person who should be regarded as a force to be reckoned with.

For various reasons younger people nowadays tend to have received less formal instruction in grammar, punctuation and spelling than was the case in earlier decades. This can probably be attributed, in part at least, to changing educational systems. No one is suggesting that you go out and take a crash course in these subjects before writing a letter, but if the letter is really important to you it is worth referring to reference books, such as a dictionary or a book on English usage. It is also worth doing a rough draft of the letter so that you can check it for errors, or even ask someone to check it for you.

Style

As far as possible it is best to write in a style that seems natural to you as you are writing it. People who are nervous of writing are quite frequently advised to try and write as they speak, and it is particularly true of personal letters to close friends and family that the letters will be more appreciated if you write in this way. The letter will then reflect your personality and make them feel that it has brought you almost physically closer to them.

Writing as you speak, however, may not be such good advice if you are writing a formal business letter, especially if you have a very informal style of speaking. Unless you are used to occasions on which you are required to use reasonably formal English—occasions on which you have to speak in public for example—it is best not to take the 'write as you speak' maxim too literally. If you do you may end up with rather a conversational letter that does not suit your purpose.

On the other hand, you should not try to adopt an extremely formal, rather stuffy style with which you do not feel comfortable and which you really do not understand. Such a style often involves rather difficult or even old-fashioned words that you would find difficult to use with any degree of expertise. If you adopt a style that is excessively formal, your letter will end up seeming stiff and stilted and totally unnatural.

The best advice is to try and be yourself as much as possible without being too conversational. Try reading the letter aloud to make sure that it sounds natural to you and is a true record of what you want to say and how you want to say it.

You should aim for simplicity and you should also aim for clarity. This often means aiming for brevity. Complicated, convoluted ways of saying something should be avoided in favour of the straightforward. Very long, complex sentences should also be avoided since it is all too easy to get lost, either when you are writing them or when you are reading them.

As has just been mentioned, brevity should be one of your major aims when writing business letters. People in general do not have the time, inclination or the concentration span to read great screeds. When faced with a very long letter they will almost certainly never get to the end, and they may not even begin. A page and a half of A4 paper is about the extent that will be tolerated.

Overall brevity is to be praised, as long as you get in everything that absolutely has to be said. However, it is worth trying to avoid having all your sentences very short. Although this makes for clarity it also makes for rather a staccato style, which can sound rather sharp. Such a style is undoubtedly better in a business letter than a convoluted one involving very long sentences but it is better to aim for a middle way with some short sentences and some rather longer ones. This will help to create a feeling of continuity.

Another feature of letter-writing that makes for smoother flowing prose is the avoidance of sentences that all begin with the same word. If the sentences are also short this can emphasize the staccato style created by a series of short sentences. This avoidance of sentences beginning with the same word is very difficult to achieve, particularly if that word is 'I'. It is sometimes almost impossible to avoid this and one just has to live with it.

The layout of paragraphs has been dealt with to some extent in the previous chapter and they are also dealt with under the section on grammar in this chapter. Under this section on style it should be mentioned that if you want to avoid a very staccato style you should try not to use a series of one-sentence paragraphs.

When you are writing a business letter you are not writing a literary work and so its content is more important than the style. However, you may as well aim to be as stylish as possible, which may enhance the impression that your letter will create.

Grammar

Grammar is much too complex a subject to cover in any detail within the scope of this book. However, some basic grammatical information likely to be useful to letter-writers is given below.

Sentence

If you wish to create a favourable impression in your business letters it is absolutely essential to write in sentences. A sentence begins with a capital letter and ends with a full stop—or occasionally with an exclamation or question mark. It is a group of words that can stand alone and make sense and contains a subject and a predicate.

For example, *The boy broke the window* is a sentence, *the boy* being the subject and *broke a window* being the predicate. On the other hand, *Seeing things* is not a sentence since there is no subject and the words cannot stand alone and make sense without any other information. Likewise, *Boys and girls* is not a sentence, since the group of words cannot stand alone and make sense without any other information and there is no predicate. *The boy broke the window* is called a simple sentence since it contains only one clause.

There are other kinds of sentence. One of these is called a compound sentence. This consists of two clauses joined by a word like *and* or *but*, as *We went out early and we came back late*.

Another kind of sentence is called a complex sentence. This consists of two or more clauses joined by a word such as *when*, *since*, *although*, *where*, etc, which are called conjunctions. Examples include *Since he is not in the office he cannot give you a reply*, *When he sees her he will be surprised*, and *The party is going ahead although it is raining*.

Clause

There is more than one kind of clause. One kind, called a main clause, is rather like a sentence, in that it could stand alone, except that it is joined to another clause by a word called a conjunction. Thus, *He went to the city and he stayed there for a few days,* is a sentence made up of two main clauses.

Another kind of clause is called a subordinate clause. This kind of clause occurs in a sentence with a main clause. Thus in the sentence, *They will leave when the others arrive*, the main clause is *They will leave* and the subordinate clause is *when the others arrive*.

It is possible to place a subordinate clause before the main clause, as *Since he is too young to go to school he goes to a playgroup*. This is a way of varying your prose to make it more interesting and avoids beginning all the sentences with the same word.

There is much more to learn about clauses but this is not a study of grammar. The subject has been raised here only because knowing what a clause is helps one to understand what a sentence is. All writers of correct English, writers of letters included, require to know what a sentence is in order that they may write clearly and creatively.

Paragraph

A paragraph is a subdivision of a piece of prose. It should deal with one particular point or theme of the writer's argument and, when this has finished, a new paragraph should be started. Unfortunately it is not as simple as this.

Firstly, if the paragraph is very long, it can be difficult for the reader to make his or her way through it. Secondly, a very long paragraph can be very off-putting visually to the would-be reader. It is better to try to subdivide your point or argument and go for shorter paragraphs. This is true of all forms of prose and it is exceptionally true of letters.

Writers are usually advised to avoid one-sentence paragraphs and letter-writers aiming for a degree of style in their prose should follow this advice. In a letter that is purely for information, however, this is sometimes difficult to achieve, nevertheless letters should not be padded out unnecessarily simply to avoid one-sentence paragraphs.

Verb

It is important in any piece of business writing that is designed to create a favourable impression that the right part of the verb is used. A verb is often described to children as being the 'doing' word in a sentence. This is rather simplistic, but it does give the right idea since the verb is the word in a sentence that is most concerned with the action. We have seen above that a sentence is made up of a subject and predicate, as *The boy broke the window*, with *broke the window* being the predicate. The most important word in the predicate is the verb, i.e. *broke*.

There are several complex issues relating to verbs,

former is dealt with under the section o
rther on in this chapter. The latter is dea
pendix B at the back of the book.

r noun is one that refers to one thing or per
car, hat, garden and mouse are singula
gular nouns or pronouns are accompanied by
he singular form. Thus we write, The little gir
r, He does not know, and She has money. We
The little girls take sugar, They do not know
have money. In these sentences takes, does and
gular forms of verbs and take, do and have are
ns of the verb.

oun is one that refers to more than one thing or
hus, cars, hats and gardens are plural nouns.
ns form their plural form by adding s to the sin-
n, as in the case of car/cars. However, singular
t end in a consonant followed by y end in -ies.
find fairies from fairy and story from stories but
from monkey.
hat end in o can cause problems. Some of these,
tomato/tomatoes and potato/potatoes, add -es,
others simply add s. Others again can take either
e best thing to do is to consult a reliable diction-
se its recommendation.
lural forms of nouns are formed irregularly, as
ice and foot/feet. Some of these are listed in
x B at the back of the book.

which will not be discussed here as you will be able to write a letter without a detailed knowledge of them. Knowing something about verbs, however, will help you avoid making some errors.

Tense is an important feature of verbs. It shows the time at which the action of the verb takes place and there are several tenses. The most basic of these will be mentioned here.

First is the *present tense* which describes an action now going on or a state that is now existing, for example, *We walk to work*, or *The world is round*. The form of the present tense changes in a way that the past does not, the form changing according to *person* (see below). Thus, in the case of the verb *fear* the first person singular (or I) is accompanied by the verb form *fear*, but the third person singular form (he, she or it) is accompanied by the verb form *fears* and the third person plural (they) is accompanied by the verb form *fear*.

A variation on the present tense is the *continuous present tense* or the *progressive present tense*. This is formed with a part of the verb *to be*, for example, *We were walking to work*, and *The wheel is turning*.

The *future tense* refers to an action or state that will take place at some time in the future. It is now mostly formed with *will*, with *shall* being used for emphasis, as in *They will be here tomorrow* and *They shall be here tomorrow*.

The *past tense* refers to an action or state that has taken place before the present time, as in *We walked to work*, and *The car was old*. How to form the past tense of verbs can cause problems for letter-writers as it is easy to go wrong.

In the case of what are known as *regular verbs,* then -ed

is added to the base form of the verb. Thus, the past tense of *look* is *looked* and the past tense of *fear* is *feared*.

In the case of *irregular verbs* the issue is not so simple since they do not simply add -*ed* to the base form to make the past tense, as *dug* from *dig* and *heard* from *hear*. A list of some irregular verbs and their past tenses is given in Appendix B at the rear of the book.

The perfect tense is another tense that refers to the past. It is formed by using the verb *to have* and the *past participle*, as *We have worked hard*, and *They have looked everywhere*. It is mentioned here because, as is the case with the past tense, problems can arise in forming it.

In the case of what are known as *regular verbs*, the *past tense* is formed by adding -*ed* to the base form of the verb. In the case of *irregular verbs*, they are formed in various ways, sometimes along the lines of the *past tense*, as in *They have dug the garden* and *We have heard the news*. A list of some irregular verbs and their past participles are given in Appendix B at the rear of the book.

A major problem with the past tense and the past participle of irregular verbs is that they are not always the same. It is quite easy to get them wrong. For example, the past tense of the verb *to see* is *saw* while the past participle of the verb *to see* is *seen*. Thus it is correct to write, *We saw our friends yesterday* and *We have seen many houses today*.

The *present participle* is used in the forming of the *continuous present* or progressive present tense and ends in -*ing*. The -*ing* is added to the base form of the verb although often a final letter *e* from the base form

is omitted before the -*ing* is
Sometimes a final letter in
fore the -*ing* is added, as *h*
with in the section on spellin

Another spelling problem
tion with forming the past t
verbs. Some regular verbs d
the -*ed* and this issue is discu
this chapter in the section on

The infinitive form of the v
form of the verb without any
or person. Thus the infinitive

Noun

A noun indicates the name
From the point of view of lette
things that you most need to kr
they are common or proper nou
plurals.

Most nouns are *common no*
names of ordinary, everyday no
are spelt with a lower-case lett
table. *Proper nouns* are the na
things or particular individuals
eral terms. These are spelt wi
tralia, *Rome*, *Everest*, *Mary* and

Forming plurals of nouns ca
lems. Most nouns simply add *s*
car/cars, *gate/gates* and *brick/b*
lems when nouns end in -*y* and
some nouns simply have irreg

mice. Th
Plurals f
with in A

Singular
A singul
son. Thu
nouns. Si
verbs in
takes sug
also writ
and *The*
has are s
plural fo

Plural
A plural
person.
Most no
gular fo
nouns th
Thus we
monkeys
Nouns
such as
whereas
form. T
ary and
Other
mouse/
Appen

A plural noun should be accompanied by the plural form of the verb where this is relevant. Thus we write, *They live near us* and *He lives near us*.

Number
Number is a classification in grammar that consists of Singular and Plural (see above).

Person
In grammar there are three persons. *First person* refers to the person who is speaking or writing when indicating himself or herself. The first person singular pronouns are *I*, *me*, *myself* and *mine*, and the first person plural pronouns are *we*, *us*, *ourselves* and *ours*.

The *second person* refers to the person to whom you are talking. The second person singular pronouns are *you*, *yourself* and *yours* and the second person plural pronouns are the same.

The *third person* refers to a third party, not the speaker or the person spoken to. The third person singular pronouns are *he/she/it*, *him/her/it*, *himself/herself/itself* and *his/hers/its*, and the third person plural pronouns are *they*, *them*, *themselves* and *theirs*.

Pronoun
A *pronoun* is a word that takes the place of a noun. Pronouns can be important to letter-writers for several reasons. One is that you should avoid using the pronoun *he* when you do not mean someone of the male sex but someone in general or someone whose sex you do not know. This is regarded as being sexist. It can be difficult to avoid this

without being clumsy and using *he/she* or *he* or *she*. One possible way of avoiding this is to put in the plural if at all possible and use *they*. It is certainly an issue to be aware of.

Another is that you should be sure to get the difference between *I* and *me* correct. *I* is used when it is the *subject* of the sentence (see below) and *me* is used when it is the *object* (see below). Thus, you would write *My friends and I will be there* and *You and I should go separately* and *He invited my friends and me* and *There is very little difference between you and me*.

Another point about pronouns is that pronouns such as *either*, *neither* or *each* are regarded as being singular and so should take a singular verb, as in *It does not matter which hotel we stay at; either is quite suitable* and *She is not taking those dresses; neither is suitable*.

Preposition

A *preposition* shows how two elements in a sentence or clause relate to each other in time or space and is often quite a short word. In the sentence *The cat sat on the mat, on* is a preposition; in the sentence *She is at home, at* is a preposition; in the sentence *They left after lunch, after* is a preposition; and in the sentence *He sat between us, between* is a preposition. The element, usually a noun or pronoun, that follows a preposition is said to be *governed* by it.

What is important about prepositions from the point of view of the letter-writer is that the nouns or pronouns that follow prepositions are treated in the same way as the objects of verbs and take that form (see below). Thus, you write *between you and me* and *The book belongs to him.*

It is sometimes difficult to decide which preposition should follow certain words. If you are in doubt you should consult a reliable dictionary or usage book. This is the kind of usage that sometimes changes according to modern preference. For example, *different from* used to be the only form that was considered correct but now *different to* is considered acceptable, especially in informal English. It is, however, better to stick to *different from* in formal business letters.

Subject

The *subject* of a sentence is usually a noun or pronoun and often performs the action described by the verb. As far as nouns are concerned, these do not vary in form whether they are the subject or the object part of the predicate of a sentence. Thus, in the sentence *Boys were playing in the street*, *boys* is the subject and in the sentence *The dog bit the boys*, *boys* is the object.

When the subject of a sentence is a pronoun, the form is different from that which acts as the object or predicate of a sentence. Thus, *me*, *him*, *her* and *them* appear as objects and *I*, *he*, *she* and *they* appear as subjects. In the sentence *The man saw them*, *them* is the object form, whereas in the sentence *They saw the man*, *they* is the subject form.

Object

The object is usually a noun or pronoun and is the part of the sentence that often has the action performed on it and is part of the predicate. Nouns do not vary in form according to whether they are the subjects or objects of sentences but pronouns do. For further information on this, see *subject* immediately above. This point is of particular importance since so many people get it wrong when they are using *I* and *me*. *My husband and I* is correct and *between you and me* is correct.

Adjective

An adjective is a word that describes or gives information about a noun. Thus, *red*, *large* and *comfortable* are adjectives.

The *comparative* forms of adjectives can cause some problems. Many of them take their comparative forms by adding *-er* as in *brave/braver*, *short/shorter*, *mad/madder*, and *clever/cleverer*. In the case of longer adjectives, especially those with three or more syllables, as *comfortable*, the comparative is formed by using *more*, as in *more comfortable*.

The *superlative* forms of adjectives follow the same rules as the comparative forms except that they add *-est* instead of *-er* and *most* instead of *more*.

Some adjectives have irregular comparative forms and superlative forms.

These are:

adjective	comparative	superlative
good	better	best
bad	worse	worst
little	less	least
many	more	most

Adverb

An adverb is a word that modifies or adds to our information about a verb. Thus, in the sentence *He ran quickly*, *quickly* is an adverb and in the sentence *He ran fast*, *fast* is an adverb.

Many adverbs end in *-ly* and many of them cause spelling difficulties. If you are unsure of any of them it is best to consult a dictionary. It should be noted that in most adjectives ending in *-y* the *-y* changes to *-i* before *-ly* is added, as *happy/happily* and *busy/busily*.

Conjunction

Conjunctions join units of language. Co-ordinating conjunctions join units of equal status, such as two words or two main clauses. Thus, *and* is a co-ordinating conjunction in *bread and butter* and in *We asked for some water and we got it*. Subordinating conjunctions join a main clause and a subordinate or dependent clause. Thus, *because* is a subordinating conjunction in *We left early because it started to rain*.

Punctuation

An incorrectly punctuated letter will create almost as bad an impression as a badly spelt or ungrammatical one. If you master a few rules you will be able to punctuate correctly and avoid creating an unfavourable impression on the recipient of your letter.

Full stop

A full stop, also known as a point or period, is a punctuation mark consisting of a small dot. Its main use is to end a sentence but it is also found in decimal values, for example, *4.5 metres*, and in some abbreviations.

Abbreviations involving initial capital letters do not usually nowadays have full stops, as *BBC, USA, TUC* and they should definitely not be used if one or some of the initial letters do not belong to a full word, as *TV*.

Question mark

If the sentence is a question rather than a statement it should not end with a full stop but with a question mark, as *Where did he go?* Questions can consist of one word, as *Why?* A question mark is sometimes known as a query.

Exclamation mark

If the sentence is a statement that is called out with strong feeling of some kind then an exclamation mark can be used instead of a full stop, as *What a nerve he has!* Exclamations can be one word, as *Help!*

You should be careful not to overuse exclamation marks. They can be effective occasionally but do not pepper your letter with them.

Capital letter

Capital letters are the opposite of lower-case or small letters. They are sometimes known as upper-case letters.

The first word of a sentence begins with a capital letter, as *The women were watching the children.*

The first letter of a name or proper noun is also always a capital letter, as *South America, Rome, Aunt Mary, Westminster Abbey, October, Easter* and *Monday*.

Nouns that are registered trademarks should also be

spelt with an initial capital letter, as *Jacuzzi* and *Filofax*, but if a verb is formed from a noun that is a trademark the verb begins with a lower-case letter. Thus, although the noun *Hoover* is spelt with a capital letter, being a trademark, the verb is spelt *hoover.*

Comma

As the present fashion is to punctuate as little as possible the comma is not used nearly as much as it used to be. However, there are still some cases where commas should always be used.

The individual items in a series of three or more items should be separated by commas. There is not usually a comma before *and* in such a list unless there is room for confusion. Thus, *We have to buy milk, bread, jam and sugar*, but *In the pub they served ham salad, shepherd's pie, fish and chips, and omelette.* The presence of the two *ands* in the latter sentence makes it advisable to put a comma before the *and* of the list to avoid confusion.

Commas are also used to separate off a phrase or clause that is naturally cut off from the rest of a sentence, almost if it were an aside, as in *His mother, who was of Irish extraction, was very superstitious.* In such a sentence the part in commas could be removed without altering the basic meaning.

Phrases or clauses, other than the main clause, or adverbs at the beginning of a sentence are often separated off by a comma, especially if the phrase or clause is reasonably long, as in *Since you are so interested in finding out about his job, you ask him* and *However, you are free to apply again.* As far as you are concerned it is possible to use some of your judgement and intuition. If you think something at the beginning of a sentence, other than the main clause, is long enough or separate enough to deserve a comma, then put one in. But use commas sparingly.

Commas are always used to separate off terms of address, interjections or tags from the rest of the sentence, as *Please come this way, Mrs Brown, and I shall tell the doctor that you are here*, and *It's cold today, isn't it?*

Colon

The colon (:) is a punctuation mark that is used in a sentence to explain, clarify, interpret or amplify what has gone before it, as in *The standard of school work here is very high: it is almost university standard.*

It is also used to introduce lists or long quotations, as in *The school has sent a list of things that John needs for next term: blazer, two pairs of trousers, three shirts, sweater, black shoes, sports clothes and leisure wear.*

The colon is very much like the dash but is used in more formal contexts.

Semi-colon

The semi-colon (;) is a formal and now rather rare form of punctuation. It is mainly used between clauses that are not joined by any form of conjunction, as *We had hoped for victory; sadly this did not materialize.*

It is also used to form subsets in a long list or series of names, as in *The young woman wants to be a journalist and has applied to newspapers worldwide. She has con-*

tacted 'The Times' in London; 'The Washington Post' in Washington; 'The Globe and Mail' in Toronto; 'The Age' in Melbourne; 'The Tribune' in Chicago.

Dash

The dash is a punctuation mark in the form of a short line that indicates a short break in the continuity of a sentence, as in *I was amazed when he turned up at the meeting—I thought he was still abroad.* In such a case it serves much the same purpose as brackets, except that it is frequently considered more informal. The dash is sometimes found in pairs to indicate a break in a sentence, as in *We could only hope—hope and pray—that they would reach the children in time.* It should be used sparingly, especially in writing formal pieces of prose, such as business letters. Depending on it too much can lead to careless writing, with ideas set down at random rather than in a considered order.

The dash can also be used to introduce a statement that explains or amplifies something that has been said, as in *The burglars removed everything of value from the house—silver, jewellery, paintings, hi-fi system, television and computer.* It can also be used to summarize what has gone before, as in *Disease, poverty, ignorance—these are the problems that we are trying to overcome.* In this context it is a more informal version of the colon.

Brackets

Brackets are used to enclose information that is in some way additional to the main statement. The information so enclosed is called *parenthesis* and the pair of brackets enclosing it can be known as *parentheses*. The information that is enclosed in the brackets is purely supplementary or explanatory in nature and could be removed without changing the overall basic meaning or grammatical completeness of the statement. Brackets, like commas and dashes, interrupt the flow of the main statement, but they indicate a more definite or clear-cut interruption. The fact that they are more visually obvious emphasizes this.

Material within brackets can be one word, as in *In a local wine bar we had some delicious crêpes (pancakes)* and *They didn't have the chutzpah (nerve) to challenge her.* It can also take the form of dates, as in *Robert Louis Stevenson (1850–94) is considered to be the master of the romantic adventure novel.*

The material within brackets can also take the form of a phrase, as in *They served lasagne (a kind of pasta) and some delicious veal* and *They were drinking Calvados (a kind of brandy made from apples)* or in the form of a clause, as in *We were to have supper (or so they called it) later in the evening* and *They went for a walk round the loch (as a lake is called in Scotland) before making their departure.*

It can also take the form of a complete sentence, as in *He was determined (we don't know why) to tackle the problem alone* and *She made it clear (nothing could be more clear) that she was not interested in the offer.* Sentences that appear in brackets in the middle of a sentence are not usually given an initial capital letter or a full stop, as in *They very much desired (she had no idea why) to purchase her house.* If the material within brackets comes at the end of a sentence the full stop comes outside the second bracket, as in *For some rea-*

son we agreed to visit her at home (we had no idea where she lived).

If the material in the brackets is a sentence which comes between two other sentences it is treated like a normal sentence with an initial capital letter and a closing full stop, as in *He never seems to do any studying. (He is always either asleep or watching television.) Yet he does brilliantly in his exams.* Punctuation of the main statement is unaffected by the presence of the brackets and their enclosed material, except that any punctuation that would have followed the word before the first bracket follows the second bracket, as in *He lives in a place (I am not sure exactly where), that is miles from anywhere.*

There are various shapes of brackets. Round brackets are the most common type. Square brackets are sometimes used to enclose information that is contained inside other information already in brackets, as in *(Christopher Marlowe [1564-93] was a contemporary of Shakespeare)* or in a piece of writing where round brackets have already been used for some other purpose. Thus, in a dictionary if round brackets are used to separate off the pronunciation, square brackets are sometimes used to separate off the etymologies.

Apostrophe

Apostrophe is a form of punctuation that is mainly used to indicate possession. Many spelling errors centre on the position of the apostrophe in relation to *s*.

Possessive nouns are usually formed by adding *'s* to the singular noun, as in *the girl's mother*, and *Peter's car*; by adding an apostrophe to plural nouns that end in *s*, as in all *the teachers' cars*; by adding *'s* to irregular plural nouns that do not end in *s*, as in *women's shoes*.

In the possessive form of a name or singular noun that ends in *s*, *x* or *z*, the apostrophe may or may not be followed by *s*. In words of one syllable the final *s* is usually added, as in *James's house*, *the fox's lair*, *Roz's dress*. The final *s* is most frequently omitted in names, particularly in names of three or more syllables, as in *Euripides' plays*. In many cases the presence or absence of final *s* is a matter of convention.

The apostrophe is also used to indicate omitted letters in contracted forms of words, as in *can't* and *you've*. They are sometimes used to indicate missing century numbers in dates, as in the *'60s and '70s*, but are not used at the end of decades, etc, as in *1960s*, not '1960's'.

Generally apostrophes are no longer used to indicate omitted letters in shortened forms that are in common use, as in *phone* and *flu*.

Apostrophes are often omitted wrongly in modern usage, particularly in the media and by advertisers, as in 'womens hairdressers' (*women's hairdressers*), 'childrens helpings' (*children's helpings*). In addition, apostrophes are frequently added erroneously, as in 'potato's for sale' (*potatoes for sale*) and 'Beware of the dog's' (*Beware of the dogs*). This is partly because people are unsure about when and when not to use them and partly because of the modern tendency to punctuate as little as possible.

Inverted Commas
These are used to indicate reported speech, being placed

around the direct words that someone has said. Reported speech is rare in the writing of formal letters.

Inverted commas are also sometimes used in the titles of books, plays, films, etc, as *'Bleak House'*, *'The Merchant of Venice'*, and *'The Silence of the Lambs'*. They can also be used to emphasize or draw attention to a particular word, sentence or phrase in a piece of writing, as *She wants to know how to spell 'picknicked'*.

Spelling

It is extremely important that business letters and more formal personal letters are spelt correctly. A list of some words that are frequently misspelt is given in Appendix C at the rear of the book, but you should also make sure that you have a reliable dictionary to hand so that you can check those words about which you are unsure. It is often said that there is no point in looking up a dictionary to find out how to spell a word since you have to know how to spell it in order to be able to look it up. This is not in fact the case as you often know roughly how to spell the word and you can usually find it by trial and error.

Whether to double a consonant or not before adding an ending can cause a lot of difficulty. Here are a few rules to guide you.

In words of one syllable ending in a single consonant preceded by a single vowel, the consonant is doubled when an ending starting with a vowel is added, as in *drop* and *dropped*, *pat* and *patting* and *rub* and *rubbing*.

In words of more than one syllable that end in a single consonant preceded by a single vowel, the consonant is doubled if the stress is on the last syllable, as in *begin* and *beginning, occur* and *occurring, prefer* and *pre-ferred, refer* and *referring,* and *commit* and *committed.*

In similar words where the stress is not on the last sylla-ble, the consonant does not double, as in *bigot* and *bigoted* and *develop* and *developed.*

Exceptions to this rule include words ending in *l.* The *l* doubles even in cases where the last syllable containing it is unstressed, as in *travel* and *travelled. Worship,* in which the stress is on the first syllable, is also an exception, as in *worshipped.*

Words that end in *-ible* and *-able* cause difficulty also, as it is often not easy to decide which of these endings to use. A list of adjectives ending in *-able* and a list of adjectives ending in *-ible* which are liable to be spelt wrongly appear in Appendix C at the rear of the book.

Word processors and home computers often have a spelling check so that you can make sure that your piece of typing is correctly spelt. The spelling list on some of these machines, however, is not very comprehensive, and the word you wish to check may not be on it. Furthermore, you can end up with the wrong spelling even if you have checked it. A simple word processor system will accept a word if it is a correctly spelt word even if it is not the right word in the context. For example, it would accept *there shoes* when the phrase should be *their shoes* because *there* is a word, although not the correct word in the context.

Language and vocabulary

In writing letters, especially business letters or formal per-sonal letters, you should avoid slang words and words that are exceptionally colloquial. Colloquial words tend to be used in informal or conversational English; spoken English and written English being not always the same in style and language. For example, we use contracted forms of several words in spoken English but these forms should be avoided in written formal English. Thus, *can't, won't, isn't, we'll, I'm*, and so on, are all very well in conversation, and even in informal written English, but they should be avoided in formal written English. Also to be avoided are jargon words, words that are technical or specialized and used by a particular group of people, such as scientists or doctors. They are acceptable in letters between people of the same group who will understand them, but not to anyone else.

On the other hand, you should not try to use very formal words or very formal constructions, especially if you do not understand how to use them properly. There used to be a number of very formal conventions used in the writing of business letters, as in *Re your letter of the 17th ult.*, but these are now rare and considered unnecessarily stuffy and old-fashioned. Try to keep your English as natural as possible.

Try to avoid using too many clichés, although this can be difficult, especially when you are writing personal letters in which it is not easy to find the right thing to say, such as letters of sympathy to the bereaved. Clichés are common, overworked phrases that all too easily come to our minds without our having to think about them. They include *in this day and age, all's well that ends well, at the end of the day* and *only time will tell*. It is almost impossible to avoid clichés completely, but you should try to avoid over-using them.

When writing formal letters it is always useful to keep a dictionary near to hand. If you have any doubts about the meaning of a word you should look it up rather than risk the embarrassment of using it in the wrong context.

Chapter 5

Content

The content of your letter, of course, depends on what message you want to get across and on the circumstances in which you find yourself. Some sample letters have been included in this chapter as guidelines only rather than to be copied. They will give you a general indication as to what is appropriate in certain situations.

For the most part they are business letters or formal personal letters from private individuals. People working for organizations, or representing them, should have guidelines already set down and may have to follow company policy over certain matters relating to correspondence.

For example, there may be an established procedure for dealing with complaints. One piece of advice is relevant to them, that is, reply promptly and be polite. Nothing annoys someone who is already annoyed more than receiving a very much delayed reply to a letter of complaint, receiving an offhand or aggressive letter or, worse, receiving no reply at all. Remember the old adage about the customer always being right—whether or not this is in fact the case.

Informal personal letters have not been dealt with here

simply because they are so personal. If you are writing a
love letter to someone you should not really need help
from a stranger with the content, although it is as well to
heed the advice in the rest of the book as to presentation
and style in such letters if you want to create a good impression, especially if the letter is being written quite
early in a relationship.

If you are away from home and living somewhere from
which it is impossible or expensive to telephone, you will
almost certainly resort to letter-writing to keep in touch
with your close family. Your problem is more likely to
be how to fit in all you want to say. The difficulty is
getting down to making a start. After that the words
will flow.

To send or not to send?

Far more letters are composed in the head than ever make
their way on to paper. This can be a bad thing, probably a
result of inertia, although we usually call it lack of time.
You may have missed the ideal job because you failed to
write a letter of application before the deadline date. You
may have offended someone for life because you were a
guest in her house and never quite got round to writing to
say thank you. You may be surrounded with a whole series of faulty goods because you somehow never found
the time and energy to write a letter of complaint seeking
a replacement or refund. We are all guilty of this kind of
inertia.

In the case of personal letters that we never get
around to sending, we are frequently saved by the greetings card. They often prove to be a great boon and they let

people know that we are thinking of them without us having the to find the time and make the effort to write a letter.

However, there are some situations where not writing can be a good thing. There are many occasions on which you should ask yourself 'Should I really send this letter?' It is all very well to write a letter to get some strong emotion out of your system but once you have put it in the postbox it is too late. There is no point in changing your mind then. You may consider waylaying the postman as he empties the box in an effort to retrieve the letter but he will be unable to help. Once a letter has gone into a post box or into a post office it has irretrievably started on its journey to the recipient.

Writing such a letter is absolutely fine if you find that it releases an emotion, such as pent-up rage. However, it is often more prudent to leave letters like than in your head. Although sometimes the act of putting what you feel on paper, even if you do not post it, helps you get the whole thing out of your system faster and more effectively.

The best thing to do with a letter like this is to burn it or otherwise dispose of it immediately. It may seem like good advice to sleep on it, but it is better to sleep on the problem before you actually write the letter than to write the letter and get it all ready for the post before retiring for the night. Some helpful member of your household might decide to post it for you, not knowing the explosive nature of its contents.

There are various situations in which we may write letters that we should never post. A common example is the one that we may write after a disagreement with, or a reprimand from, the boss or management at work. In the heat of the moment we may decide that we do not want or need to work for them and write a letter of resignation telling them just what they can do with their job. Simply writing the letter can bring us back to a sense of reality as well as releasing our pent-up rage. We then reflect on the fact that there are not many jobs around at the moment and that, anyhow, we quite like our present job and the boss is not that bad. Such a letter of resignation written in the heat of the moment should never be sent. If you are dead set on resigning, then the letter indicating this should be written in a state of calmness after much thought and preferably after securing another job.

Your relationship with a neighbour may be preserved or at least prevented from getting any worse by one of these unsent letters. If the people next door have a tree that is blocking the light to your dining-room window, a dog that keeps digging up your roses or a teenage son who insists on playing his stereo at top volume into the early hours of the morning—or all three—you could be excused for feeling absolutely furious.

You may feel like going round to see them in a towering rage and shouting abuse at them, threatening them with the law or even punching them on the nose, but all of these courses of action are unwise. Getting involved with the law is an expensive business and physical violence will only land you in trouble. Verbal abuse may forever damage relations with your neighbours and they may be with you for some time, with many opportunities for getting back at you. Nor it is a good idea to lift the phone and scream inarticulate abuse at them by that means. It is far better to write a letter in your head or on paper, provided that the latter is torn up, to get rid of your rage and then go round in a state of calm to try to reason with them.

There are several situations of a more personal nature in which the unsent letter can be a preserver of relationships and peace. Someone who has just had a row with her fiancé may feel a great need to lift the phone and itemize what she sees as his many faults in a furious, hysterical and practically incoherent voice, ending by saying that he can come and collect the engagement ring because she certainly does not want it. The outcome of such a response to a row can be a good one in that the fiancé may forgive the detailed onslaught on his character, may even humbly agree with it, and come rushing round, not to collect the ring but to make up the quarrel. However, he may decide that he does not want to marry someone who is capable of such abuse and lack of restraint and simply ask for the ring to be put in the post.

The truly impetuous will probably not heed such advice, but here again, the unsent letter would have been a safer bet. All the criticism could have been poured on to paper in the most furious and hysterical way and no harm done, as long as the paper was torn up afterwards.

Of course such letters are a good thing only if they are not sent. The danger is that they will be sent, not accidentally as was described above, but deliberately in a fit of passion that will later be regretted. Indeed people of a certain temperament should ignore the advice of setting their wrath down on paper. They are the kind of people who approach all areas of life in a spirit of great, almost uncontrollable, impetuosity and always act before they think.

Those who routinely experience the more extreme form of this impulsiveness are almost certainly going to take some form of action if they are experiencing great emotions. It is simply a question of damage limitation, of which course of action will cause the least permanent damage. The reaction of most people of this temperament is to use the quickest and most expedient method of doing anything and so they are very likely to reach for the telephone and hurl abuse down it. This is better than writing a letter, because a letter is a more permanent record of abuse and so likely to cause more ill-feeling.

All of us at some time in our lives find it necessary to write a letter that we actually send. The circumstances in which we send them tend to fall into categories, these categories being ones that are central to our lives.

Property and goods

One area of life that tends to lead us to write letters is that of possessions, whether it is property or goods that we have bought or that we are buying.

We often write to complain or to ask for damaged things to be fixed. In order to be most effective they should be brief and to the point. There is no point in going into great detail. In the case of letters of complaint they should be factual rather than emotional, and calm and restrained rather than abusive. Examples of such letters are given below.

Requests for an estimate

```
Tel:                                    Address

                                        Date


Abbeyhill Roofing Ltd
46 Abbeyhill,
Norwood
Whiteshire
NW2 4XY


Dear Sirs,
    The roof of my house was damaged in the
recent gales and the ceiling of one of the
bedrooms is now leaking. I have contacted my
insurance company and they have asked me to get
three written estimates before selecting a
contractor to carry out the work.
    I would be glad if you could inspect the
property as soon as possible and give me an
estimate. Please telephone to arrange a suitable
time if you are interested in submitting an
estimate.
    It is important that the work is carried
out urgently.


Yours sincerely,

Tom Henderson

Tom Henderson
```

Tel: Address

                                        Date

Mr Peter Glass
Blackford Kitchen Design Ltd
16 Forth Rd
Newhill
Whiteshire
NH15 3KT

Dear Mr Glass,

   I am considering installing a new kitchen in
my house. The rest of the house is quite modern
but the kitchen is very old-fashioned. It is
rather an odd shape and I shall need professional
help to plan it.

   If you are interested in discussing this
perhaps you could telephone to make an
appointment.

   I realize that it there is a considerable
amount of work to be done but the job has to be
completed before the end of July.

Yours sincerely,

John Peters

John Peters

Replies to estimates

Tel: Address

                                        Date

Mr Mark Garden
Central Construction Ltd
Craigpark
Whiteshire
CP12 8TY.

Dear Mr Garden,

   I am writing to confirm in writing my
telephone acceptance of your estimate dated 5th
March for work to the stonework of my garage.

   I understand that work will begin on 19th
March and will take about two days.

   I look forward to seeing you on the 19th.

Yours sincerely,

Ann Blackridge

Ann Blackridge

Tel: Address

                                        Date

Michael Little
Greenfingers
Landscape Gardeners
46 Station Road
Craigpark
Whiteshire
CP12 P34

Dear Michael Little,

   Thank you for submitting an estimate for
landscaping the garden at the above address and
for doing so promptly.

   Unfortunately I am writing to say that I am
not accepting your estimate. It was a good deal
higher than those that were submitted by other
firms.

Yours sincerely,

Philip Smith

Philip Smith

Complaining about poor work, goods or service

Tel: Address

                                                  Date

Mr Frank Smith
Manager
Slating and Roofing Contractors
16 Scott Street
Craigpark
Whiteshire
CP19 6KM

Dear Mr Smith,

<u>Repairs to Roof at 56 Wood Road</u>

   Your firm recently completed some repairs to
the roof of my house. I have to tell that you
that I am not at all satisfied with the work.
The first time that it rained, the ceiling in
one of the upstairs bedrooms leaked.

   I have tried without success to contact you
by telephone and left several messages with
your secretary to telephone me. I have been
forced to write since you have not returned any
of my calls.

   The faulty work must be put right as soon
as possible. Please get in touch either by
telephone or by letter to make an appointment
to come and inspect the roof and to arrange a
date for it to be put right.

I chose your firm on the personal recommendation of a friend and I am extremely disappointed to have been let down.

I look forward to hearing from you right away.

Yours sincerely,

Sarah Jones

Sarah Jones

Tel: Address

                                            Date

Dimble's Fashion Catalogue
65 Kingsway
Brownpool
Longshire
BP5 5TY

Dear Sirs,

Catalogue No. HT 2398

I have just received the dress that I ordered for my granddaughter from your catalogue on 4th May. It has not reached the standard that I have come to expect from your company.

My granddaughter tried the dress on when it arrived and I was angry and disappointed to find that the sewing on both the hem and the seam on the left-hand side was undone. In addition there is a dark stain on the white collar of the dress, suggesting that the dress has either been worn before or tried on without due care being taken.

As you can imagine my granddaughter was very upset, particularly since she had planned to wear the dress to her birthday party. There is really nothing that can compensate her for this disappointment.

I have not enclosed the dress referred to since I see no reason why I should go to any further expense by paying for packaging and postage. However, I will be glad to receive either a full refund or an undamaged dress together with instructions about returning the damaged one at your expense.

I would hope that any further orders that I place with your company will be dealt with in a more satisfactory way. Meanwhile I look forward to hearing your comments on the present situation.

Yours sincerely,

Robert Atkinson

Robert Atkinson

Tel: Address

                                              Date

Mr Pierre Bouleau,
Bon Appetit,
60 Princes Street
Brownwich
Broadshire
BR13 8FY.

Dear Pierre,

    As you know my family and I have been
regular clients of your restaurant since it
opened two years ago. Until our visit last
Saturday we had always been extremely
satisfied and had recommended it to several
of our friends.

    Unfortunately we will not be recommending
it to anyone else unless things improve
greatly since we were disappointed by both the
food and the service on our last visit. The
food we were served was not up to anything
like your previous standard and was served
cold by sullen waitresses who could not have
cared less.

    We gather from friends that you have
opened another restaurant in the area and are
spending some time concentrating on that.
However, the clients of your original
restaurant deserve attention as well —
otherwise we will go elsewhere.

I look forward to hearing your views on the subject.

Yours sincerely,

John Burns

John Burns

Tel: Address

                                            Date

Sunshine Holiday Tours Ltd
30 Dean Street
Brownwich
Broadshire
BR 15 7JX

Dear Sirs,

My wife and I booked a coach holiday through your company in August of this year. We were on a tour of the Italian lakes that started from Brownwich on 6th August.

Everything about the holiday fell short of the claims your company made in your advertising brochure. The coach was not air-conditioned and the accommodation throughout the trip was in badly-equipped rooms with poor food and poor service.

We complained to your courier several times in the course of the trip but she said that there was nothing she could do. Indeed she acted as though she could not care less.

Since this holiday was not at all up to the expected standard or to the standard advertised by you we are seeking compensation. We gather that several of the other people on the tour have also complained to you.

We look forward to hearing from you and to receiving details of your suggested compensation.

Yours sincerely,

Joan Rogers

Joan Rogers

Employment

Many of the letters that we find we have to write relate to employment. A letter of resignation is one kind of letter that we may have to write at some point in our working life, although because of the high unemployment ratio now these are much less common than they once were. Not very long ago people could resign before they found another job, safe in the knowledge that they would do so easily. Now, however, given how difficult it is to find a job, especially after a certain age, most people would not dream of resigning before they have another job. Also people tend to move around in the job market a lot less than was formerly the case, again because of lack of opportunities.

Of course, people still do resign form their jobs and when they do, many of them have to formalize this by putting the fact in writing. Here, as in the case of many business letters, you should aim for brevity. However much you hated the job or however badly you think you have been treated, you should resist the temptation to rant and rave or be abusive.

There is no point in trying to settle old scores in your letter of resignation. You may feel that it would do you a lot of good to tell your employers what they can do with their job, but you should think of the future. Even if you did not need a reference from your employers for the job that you have just obtained, you may need one in the future. Since you will have to indicate your employment record on your CV, the employers you are now leaving may be contacted in the future by prospective employers.

Then there is another point to be considered. In the case of large companies, bosses move around as well as employees. Who knows? The boss to whom you are now being abusive in writing may well one day end up as your boss again.

There is much to be said, therefore, for writing a letter of resignation that will keep relations with your ex-employers as warm as possible. If you can possibly bring yourself to do it, you should include something positive about how you feel about your years of employment with them. It may even be true.

Letters of application are much more common than letters of resignation. These take two forms—letters applying for advertised posts and letters written to investigate possible job opportunities.

The latter are mostly written by young people who are just leaving school or further education and seeking their first job. Since finding a first job is an extremely difficult task, job-seekers so doing should be prepared to bombard firms that operate in the areas in which they are most interested.

They should be prepared to be disappointed on two counts. Obviously there may be no job available and they may get a letter of rejection. Often more discouraging is the fact that they may receive no acknowledgement of their letters at all. Employers claim that they receive so many speculative letters regarding employment in their firms that they could not possibly reply to all of them. Nevertheless, it is very depressing for job-seekers to keep sending off letters and to always be met with silence.

If you are writing a letter that is not a reply to an advertisement you may well not know to whom you should send your letter. In the case of reasonably large firms you should address letters of application to the personnel manager. If the firm does not have an employee of this title the letters will be passed to the person in the company who deals with employment. Your letter should contain a CV and a brief typed letter trying to sell yourself and your skills to the firm.

If the letter is a reply to an advertisement you should obviously comply with the requests made by it. Sometimes a CV is asked for, in which case you should send a brief letter accompanying it in which you state why you are right for the job.

CVs have a distressing habit of looking remarkably similar to each other and so it is a good idea to try and personalize your letter to bring favourable attention to your application.

Both the CV and the letter should be typed unless otherwise stated. As mentioned previously, it is becoming increasingly common for firms to ask for letters of application to be handwritten. Sometimes this is because employers wish to find out, perhaps from professional graphologists, something about the character and personality of the applicant and sometimes it is because they are seeking an employee who has readily legible handwriting.

Many firms and organizations send out application forms. These can be quite challenging, especially if they ask such questions as 'Why do you want this post?' or 'What qualities do you feel you could bring to this post?' and can take considerable time to complete.

The CV has become a central part of most job applications. Given the difficulty of finding a job and the importance of presenting yourself in as positive a way as possible, many people get their CVs compiled by one of the professional agencies that have been set up to provide such a service. The CV is very important and must be correctly spelt, neatly set out and give a general air of professionalism.

There has been a recent change in attitudes to CVs. Until relatively recently it was the preferred practise to put just about everything the applicant had ever done or was ever interested in on the CV. This often made for a very long and crowded document and took a long time for prospective employers to digest. Furthermore, particularly in the case of school leavers or new graduates, many of the CVs are remarkably similar.

For these reasons there is now a tendency to keep the CV fairly brief and to treat it more as record of qualifications and employment. Employers have grown to rely more on the letter accompanying the CV than on the CV itself. Such letters are an opportunity for applicants to sell themselves to prospective employers and should be a brief account of all the features, qualifications and experience that make you ideal for the advertised post.

Resignation

```
Tel:                                Address

                                    Date


Mr Frank Brown
Personnel Manager
Lomond Financial Services
35 Milton Street
Neathing
Whiteshire
NT12 8DR


Dear Mr Brown,
    I am writing to inform you of my decision
to resign from the company. As is required by
the conditions of my contract I am giving you
four weeks' notice, which begins today.
    My reason for leaving is that I have
obtained a more senior post with Carlton
Investment Services.
    I have very much enjoyed working with Lomond
Financial Services and I shall be sorry to
leave. However, at the moment there is little
opportunity for promotion at my level and so I
feel that I must move on.


Yours sincerely,

Richard Todd

Richard Todd
```

Tel: Address

                                            Date

Mark Howe, Esq
Redford Engineering Ltd
37 Hanover Street
Brunstane
Brownshire
BT14 7WB

Dear Mr Howe,

I understand that the firm is offering early
retirement to some older employees as part of a
staff reorganization scheme. It is likely that
I shall take advantage of this offer and I
would like to receive details of the retirement
settlement.

The reason for my decision to retire early
is that my wife is in poor health and I would
like to be able to spend more time with her.

I would like to leave as soon as possible
and so I hope that we can reach agreement on a
settlement as soon as possible.

I look forward to hearing from you.

Yours sincerely,

Peter Smythe

Peter Smythe

Job Application

```
Tel:                          Address

                              Date


Ms Diane Brand,
Personnel Manager
Moneywise Insurance Ltd
47 Castle Road
Laddington
Redshire
LD3 9 RT
```

Dear Ms Brand,

I am writing in reply to your advertisement in 'The Chronicle' of 5th August for a nursery assistant in the crèche run by your firm for children of employees.

As you will see from my CV, I have just left school and am taking a year out before taking up a place at Neath Teachers' Training College. When I graduate I would like to find a post teaching younger children in the primary school and I am therefore looking for a job working with young children during my year out to gain some experience.

I am extremely interested in the advertised post and think that I have the right experience and personality for the job. Since I have three sisters who are much younger than me and several young cousins, I am used to dealing with young children. I frequently baby-sit for

my own family and also for several of our
neighbours.

I like working with children, which is why I
am making primary teaching my career. However,
I do appreciate that working with them requires
great energy, enthusiasm, initiative and
patience and I would bring all these qualities
to the post of nursery assistant.

As to leisure activities, I play the piano
and the guitar and like dancing and painting.
All these activities are useful to people who
are working with children.

References can be obtained from the head
teacher of my school, Mr Peter Sharp, and from
Ms Jean Peden, a neighbour for whom I baby-sit
frequently. Their addresses and telephone
numbers are given in my CV.
I look forward to hearing from you.

Yours sincerely,

Joanna Smart

Joanna Smart

Tel: Address

                                                  Date

Ms Esther Martin
Editorial Director
Paragon Publishing Ltd
30 Blandford Lane,
Kingsferry
Whiteshire
KF15 7KL

Dear Ms Martin

I am about to graduate from Glasburgh
University with an Honours Degree in English
Language and am interested in obtaining a post
in the publishing industry. Although I would
welcome the opportunity to work in any of the
areas of publishing I would prefer the editorial area.

Most of my family are engaged in the publishing industry in some form and I have wanted
to be in publishing since before I left school.
With that in mind I have had various temporary
jobs and periods of work experience involving
books, as you will see from my CV, which I
enclose.

Since these jobs have included work as an
assistant editor on an encyclopedia, work in
the design department of a publishing house,
work as a production assistant on a magazine
and a regular Saturday job at my local

bookseller's, I feel that I have the right
background to enter publishing. In addition, I
have been the assistant editor of our student
newspaper for two years.

My hobbies include photography and writing.
I have had several articles published in 'The
Forth Review', our local weekly newspaper,
mostly in the form of theatre reviews.

I am a good communicator and work well under
pressure. I am used to working with computers
and took a word processing course before going
to university.

I look forward to hearing from you.

Yours sincerely,

Sarah Brown

Sarah Brown

CV (Curriculum vitae)

NB It is important that these are set out neatly and attractively. Some people choose to take advantage of the potential of home computers and word processors to use a selection of type sizes and typefaces, but too much variety can be rather distracting and even ugly. The suggested CV below relates only to the content.

Name	John Smith
Address	65 Queen's Road Blackford Whiteshire BD14 7 RT
Telephone	01X1 666888
Date of birth	24 February 1951
Nationality	British
Marital status	divorced
Secondary education	1962-68 Raxworth Grammar School 25 Beach Road High Raxworth Braxshire RX4 8DG

'O' levels	English, French, Maths, Spanish, History, German, Geography, Art
'A' levels	English Grade A, French Grade B, Spanish Grade B
Further Education	1968-1971 Glasburgh University Dean Square Glasburgh Blackshire GB3 9RF
Degree	BA (Honours) French and German Upper Second class
Employment	1971-1978 Translator Publications Dept Unitech Ltd Newridge
	1978-1987 Head of Translation Publications Dept Chemec plc Birchingham

```
                        1987-1990
                        Chief Translator
                        Chemec plc
                        New York


Leisure Activities      Golf, hill-walking,
                        photography, cinema,
                        theatre-going.


Referees                Robert Adams
                        Editorial Director
                        Publications
                        Chemec plc
                        37 Sea Way
                        Brownpool
                        Newshire
                        BL5 9KL


                        Peter Schwartz
                        Head of Publications
                        Unitech Ltd
                        Newridge
                        Newshire
                        NR4 8RT
```

References

Tel: Address

                                            Date

Ms Jane White
Head Teacher
St Mark's Secondary School
5 School Lane
Stonyburn
Blackshire
SB12 7TY

Dear Ms White,

I am writing to ask if I may use you as one of my referees for a job for which I am applying. The job is clerical assistant with Global Insurance.

I left school at the end of the summer term and passed 6 GCSEs. Since then I have been working as an au pair in France.

I was a pupil at St Mark's from 1986–1992. In my last year I was in Ms Peter's form class.

I hope that you will be able to help.

Yours sincerely

Joanna Thames

Joanna Thames

Tel: Address

                                        Date

Ms Penny Main
Personnel Manager
Global Insurance
3 High Street
Stonyburn
Blackshire
SB13 9TZ

Dear Ms Main,

   Thank you for your letter of 5th September
asking for my views on the suitability of Joan
Thames for a post as clerical office with your
firm.

   I got to know Joan quite well as I took her
form for a weekly discussion group when she was
in her final year at St Mark's.

   Joan is a very honest, hard-working girl and
always tries to do her best. She is very
pleasant and polite and gets on very well with
people.

   I am sure that if you decide to employ her
she will be an asset to the firm.

Yours sincerely,

Jane White

Jane White

Tel: Address

                                            Date

Ms Jane White
Head Teacher
St Mark's Secondary School
5 School Lane
Stonyburn
Blackshire
SB13 9TZ

Dear Ms White,

   I am writing to thank you very much for
agreeing to act as one of my referees for the
post that I applied for with Global Insurance.

   I am delighted to say that I got the job and
I start at the beginning of the month.

   With many thanks for your help,

Yours sincerely,

Joanna Thames

Joanna Thames

Personal Letters

Unless we are away from home for some time it is unusual for many of us to write personal letters as the telephone is more convenient. If we want to send a friend some kind of written message, then a greetings card will usually do. However, there a few situations where a reasonably formal letter is required rather than a card.

One of these situations occurs with the death of someone we know reasonably well but who is not a close friend. In the case of close friends we would go round to see the bereaved relative, send an informal note or wait until we see them at the funeral, but in other cases, such as the death of a work colleague, it is more appropriate to send a short, reasonably formal letter.

Such letters are extremely difficult to write. Obviously the person who is going to receive it is going to be in a distressed state and it is hard to think of anything to say that will bring any kind of comfort. In fact it is almost impossible to do this, but many recipients of such letters find comfort just in the fact that people have remembered their relative and thought highly enough of him or her to write.

It is difficult to avoid clichés in letters of sympathy and condolence, but bereavement is not an area in which striving for originality is particularly appropriate. In the circumstances a few clichés are probably quite acceptable. One more thing—it is as well to set aside your typewriter or word processor. Unless your handwriting is completely illegible it is better to write, rather than type, letters of sympathy as it seems much more personal.

The other situation in which it is often better to write a personal letter rather than telephone is with letters giving thanks for gifts or for some act of kindness. Of course, it is often quite appropriate to telephone one's thanks, particularly to close friends or family members. However some people, especially older people, feel insulted if no written message of thanks is sent. You have to try and judge the preference of the person to whom you owe thanks and act accordingly.

Just as letters of bereavement require a marked degree of sensitivity, so to do letters of thanks, especially those in response to presents. Often they require a degree of tact as totally unsuitable presents often have to be acknowledged as well as acceptable ones. The problem is often one of knowing what to say about the unwanted gift without being excessively enthusiastic and so risk getting a similar gift again.

It is often difficult also to decide how to fill the space. You can keep the message brief, but you have to do better than two lines. However much or little you choose to write you might think of writing the letter by hand instead of dashing it of on your word processor. Some people, again often older people, prefer the more personal touch of the handwritten note.

Bereavement

Tel: Address

                                                  Date

Dear Mrs Hughes,

I was so sorry to hear of the sudden death of your husband. Please accept my deepest sympathy.

It is some time since I saw Peter but we were good friends when I worked with him at G& H Law's. I particularly enjoyed his good sense of humour. He could cheer us all up when we were feeling low.

He will be much missed by his colleagues at Law's and also by the community in general. He gave so much of his time to raising funds for charity.

I know that your family will be round you at this time but if there is anything I can do please do not hesitate to get in touch.

With kind regards,

Yours sincerely,

Maureen Brown

Letters of thanks

Tel: Address

                                                  Date

Dear Margaret,

Thank you very much for having me to stay over Easter. It was very kind of you to invite me and I really appreciated being part of a family again. As you know both my children are working abroad this year and I miss them.

It was very pleasant to get out of the bustle of London for a few days. I must say that you live in a very beautiful part of the world and it was good to have time to explore it. I could not believe that the weather was so warm at this time of year.

I would love to return your hospitality. If ever any of you, or preferably all of you, feel like a few days in London, just get in touch. You will be very welcome. I know you were glad to leave London for the country but it has its compensations.

With very many thanks,

Yours sincerely,

Joyce Green

Tel: *Address*

                                              Date

Dear Great-Aunt Gertrude,

I am writing to thank you very much for the birthday present that you sent me. It was kind of you to remember, although I feel that I am reaching the age when I would be better forgetting birthdays.

The silk scarf was absolutely lovely. The purple colour will go really well with my new winter coat. It needs a bright colour to cheer it up a bit.

I hope that you are well and are getting out a bit despite this depressing winter weather. When the weather improves you must think of coming up to London. Do let me know if you would like to come. We would all love to see you.

With many thanks and best wishes,

Love, Jill

These then are some of the most likely situations in which you might find yourself faced with writing letters. Obviously the wording of your own particular letters may vary from the wording of the sample letters according to the circumstances and according what you want to say. Nevertheless, they will act as a framework and give you a general idea of what is appropriate both in language and in content in certain situations.

With all business letters and formal personal letters the message remains the same. Aim for clarity, brevity, simplicity, accuracy of spelling, grammar and punctuation and neatness of presentation. With this goal in mind you will not go far wrong and you will achieve your aim of making a good impression on the recipient of your letter.

Appendix A

Some Special Forms of Address

Ambassador
opening greeting
Dear Sir —— —— *or* Sir *or* Dear Mr ——

name on envelope
His Excellency The British, *etc*, Ambassador, *or* His Excellency, Sir —— —— KCMG, or His Excellency —— —— KCMG *or* His Excellency, HM Ambassador to —— (*name of relevant country*)

Archbishop (Anglican)
opening greeting
Your Grace, Dear Lord Archbishop *or* Dear Archbishop

name on envelope
His Grace the Lord Archbishop of —— *or* The Most Rev. and Rt Hon. the Lord Archbishop of ——

Archdeacon
opening greeting Dear Archdeacon *or* Mr Archdeacon *or* Venerable Sir

name on envelope
The Venerable the Archdeacon of ——

Baron (*see also* **Life Peer**)
opening greeting
Dear Lord ——

name on envelope
The Rt Hon. the Lord —— *or* The Lord ——

Baroness (wife of **Baron**; *see also* **Life Peeress**)
opening greeting
Dear Lady ——

name on envelope
The Lady ——

Baronet
opening greeting
Dear Sir *or* Dear Sir ——

name on envelope
Sir —— ——, Bt *or* Sir —— ——, Bart.

Baronet's wife
opening greeting
Dear Lady ——

name on envelope
Lady ——

Bishop
opening greeting
Dear Lord Bishop *or* Dear Bishop

name on envelope
The Rt Rev. the Lord Bishop of ——

Bishop of London
opening greeting
Dear Lord Bishop

name on envelope
The Rt Rev. and Rt Hon. The Lord Bishop of London

Canon
opening greeting
Dear Canon *or* Reverend Sir

name on envelope
The Rev. Canon ——

Chief Rabbi
opening greeting
Dear Chief Rabbi *or* Dear Rabbi ——

name on envelope
The Chief Rabbi Dr ——

Clergyman
opening greeting
Dear Mr —— *or* (*where relevant*) Dear Father ——

name on envelope
The Rev. —— —— *or* The Reverend —— ——

Countess
opening greeting
Dear Countess of —— *or* Dear Lady ——

name on envelope
The Countess of ——

Dame
opening greeting
Dear Dame ——

name on envelope
Dame —— —— (*with appropriate decoration*)

Dean
opening greeting
Very Reverend Sir, Dear Dean *or* Dear Mr Dean

name on envelope
The Very Rev. the Dean of ——

Rural Dean
same as for clergyman

Duchess
opening greeting
Dear Duchess of —— *or* Dear Duchess

name on envelope
Her Grace The Duchess of —— *or* The Duchess of ——

Royal duchess
opening greeting
Your Royal Highness

name on envelope
Her Royal Highness The Duchess of ——

Duke
opening greeting
Dear Duke of —— *or* Dear Duke

name on envelope
His Grace the Duke of —— *or* The Duke of ——

Royal duke
opening greeting
Your Royal Highness

name on envelope
His Royal Highness The Duke of ——

Earl
opening greeting
Dear Earl of —— or Dear Lord ——

name on envelope
The Rt Hon. Earl of —— or The Earl of ——

Hon.
(= Honourable, although never written out in full)
opening greeting
Dear Mr/Mrs/Miss ——

name on envelope
The Hon. Mr/Mrs/Miss ——

Judge (Circuit)
opening greeting
Dear Judge *or* Dear Sir /Dear Madam
name on envelope
His Honour the Judge/Her Honour the Judge

Judge (High Court)
opening greeting
Dear Sir/Dear Madam

name on envelope
The Hon. Mr Justice —— /The Hon. Mrs Justice ——
/The Hon. Ms Justice ——

Knight
opening greeting
Dear Sir —— ——

name on envelope
Sir —— —— KBE

Knight's wife
opening greeting
Dear Lady ——

name on envelope
Lady ——

Life Peer
opening greeting Dear Lord ——

name on envelope
The Rt Hon. the Lord —— *or* The Lord ——

Life Peeress
opening greeting
Dear Lady ——

name on envelope
The Rt Hon. the Baroness —— *or* The Baroness —— *or*
Baroness ——

Lord Mayor

opening greeting
My Lord *or* Dear Lord Mayor

name on envelope
The Right Worshipful the Lord Mayor *but* The Rt Hon. the Lord Mayor of London, The Rt Hon. the Lord Mayor of York.

Marchioness

opening greeting
Dear Marchioness of —— *or* Dear Lady ——

name on envelope
The Marchioness of ——

Marquess

opening greeting
Dear Marquess of —— *or* Dear Lord ——

name on envelope
The Marquess of Falborough

Mayor

opening greeting
Dear Mr Mayor *or* Dear Mr ——

name on envelope
The Right Worshipful the Mayor of —— (city) *or* The Worshipful the Mayor of —— (borough, etc)

Pope

opening greeting
Your Holiness *or* Most Holy Father

name on envelope
His Holiness the Pope John XI

President of the United States
opening greeting
Dear Mr President/Dear Madam President *or* Sir/Madam

name on envelope
The President of the United States

Prime Minister
opening greeting
Dear Prime Minister *or* Dear Mr ——/Dear Mrs/
Ms ——

name on envelope
The Rt Hon. —— —— PC, MP

Prince of Wales
opening greeting
Your Royal Highness

name on envelope
His Royal Highness the Prince of Wales, *or letters should
be sent to* The Private Secretary to His Royal Highness
The Prince of Wales

Queen
opening greeting
Your Majesty or Dear Sir (to her private secretary)

name on envelope
letters should be sent to The Private Secretary to Her
Majesty the Queen

Unmarried daughter of Duke, Marquess or Earl
opening greeting
Dear Lady —— ——

name on envelope
Lady —— ——

Viscount
opening greeting
Dear Viscount —— *or* Dear Lord ——

name on envelope
The Rt Hon. the Viscount —— *or* The Viscount ——

Viscountess
opening greeting   Dear Viscountess —— *or* Dear
Lady ——

name on envelope
The Viscountess ——

Appendix B

Irregular Verbs and Nouns

Irregular verbs are verbs that do not conform to the usual pattern of verbs of adding *-ed* to the past tense and past participle. They fall into several categories.

One category concerns those which have the same form in the past tense and past participle forms as the infinitive and do not end in *-ed*, like regular verbs. These include:

infinitive	*past tense*	*past participle*
bet	bet	bet
burst	burst	burst
cast	cast	cast
cost	cost	cost
cut	cut	cut
hit	hit	hit
hurt	hurt	hurt
let	let	let
put	put	put
set	set	set
shed	shed	shed
shut	shut	shut
slit	slit	slit

split	split	split
spread	spread	spread

Some irregular verbs have two past tenses and two past participles which are the same, as in:

infinitive	*past tense*	*past participle*
burn	burned, burnt	burned, burnt,
dream	dreamed, dreamt	dreamed ,dreamt,
dwell	dwelled, dwelt	dwelled, dwelt,
hang	hanged, hung,	hanged, hung
kneel	kneeled, knelt,	kneeled, knelt
lean	leaned, leant	learned, learnt
leap	leaped, leapt,	leaped, leapt
learn	learned, learnt	learned, learnt
light	lighted, lit	lighted, lit
smell	smelled, smelt	smelled, smelt
speed	speeded, sped	speeded, sped
spill	spilled, spilt	spilled, spilt
spoil	spoiled, spoilt	spoiled, spoilt
weave	weaved, woven	weaved, woven
wet	wetted, wet	wetted, wet,

Some irregular verbs have past tenses that do not end in *-ed* and have the same form as the past participle. These include:

infinitive	*past tense*	*past participle*
bend	bent	bent
bleed	bled	bled
breed	bred	bred
build	built	built
cling	clung	clung

dig	dug	dug
feel	felt	felt
fight	fought	fought
find	found	found
flee	fled	fled,
fling	flung	flung
get	got	got
grind	ground	ground
hear	heard	heard
hold	held	held
keep	kept	kept
lay	laid	laid
lead	led	led
leave	left	left
lend	lent	lent
lose	lost	lost
make	made	made
mean	meant	meant
meet	met	met
pay	paid	paid
rend	rent	rent
say	said	said
seek	sought	sought
sell	sold	sold
send	sent	sent
shine	shone	shone
shoe	shod	shod
sit	sat	sat
sleep	slept	slept
slide	slid	slid
sling	slung	slung

slink	slunk	slunk
spend	spent	spent
stand	stood	stood
stick	stuck	stuck
sting	stung	stung
strike	struck	struck
string	strung	strung
sweep	swept	swept
swing	swung	swung
teach	taught	taught
tell	told	told
think	thought	thought
understand	understood	understood
weep	wept	wept
win	won	won
wring	wrung	wrung

Some irregular verbs have regular past tense forms but two possible past participles, one of which is regular. These include:

infinitive	*past tense*	*past participle*
mow	mowed	mowed, mown
prove	proved	proved, proven
sew	sewed	sewn, sewed
show	showed	showed, shown
sow	sowed	sowed, sown
swell	swelled	swelled, swollen

Some irregular verbs have past tenses and past participles that are different from each other and different from the infinitive. These include:

infinitive	past tense	past participle
arise	arose	arisen
awake	awoke	awoken
bear	bore	borne
begin	began	begun
bid	bade	bidden
bite	bit	bitten
blow	blew	blown
break	broke	broken
choose	chose	chosen
do	did	done
draw	drew	drawn
drink	drank	drunk
drive	drove	driven
eat	ate	eaten
fall	fell	fallen
fly	flew	flown
forbear	forbore	forborne
forbid	forbade	forbidden
forgive	forgave	forgiven
forget	forgot	forgotten
forsake	forsook	forsaken
freeze	froze	frozen
forswear	forswore	foresworn
give	gave	given
go	went	gone
grow	grew	grown
hew	hewed	hewn
hide	hid	hidden
know	knew	known
lie	lay	lain

ride	rode	ridden
ring	rang	rung
saw	sawed	sawn
see	saw	seen
rise	rose	risen
shake	shook	shaken
shrink	shrank	shrunk
slay	slew	slain
speak	spoke	spoken
spring	sprang	sprung
steal	stole	stolen
stink	stank	stunk
strew	strewed	strewn
stride	strode	stridden
strive	strove	striven
swear	swore	sworn
swim	swam	swum
take	took	taken
tear	tore	torn
throw	threw	thrown
tread	trod	trodden
wake	woken	woke
wear	wore	worn
write	written	wrote

Irregular Plural Nouns

Irregular plurals refer to the plural form of nouns that do not form their plural in the regular way. Most nouns in English add -s to the singular form to form the plural form, as in *boy* to *boys*.

Some add -es to the singular form to form the plural, as

in *church* to *churches*. Nouns ending in a consonant followed by *-y* have *-ies* as a regular plural ending. Thus *fairy* becomes *fairies* and *berry* becomes *berries*. The foregoing are all examples of *regular plurals*.

Irregular plurals include words that are different in form from the singular forms and do not simply add an ending. These include *men* from *man*, *women* from *woman* and *mice* from *mouse*.

Some irregular plurals are formed by changing the vowel of the singular forms, as in *feet* from *foot*, *geese* from *goose* and *teeth* from *tooth*.

Some irregular plural forms are formed by adding *-en*, as *oxen* from *ox* and *children* from *child*.

Some nouns ending in *-f* form plurals in *-ves*, as in *loaf* to *loaves*, *half* to *halves*, *wife* to *wives* and *wolf* to *wolves*, but some have alternative endings, as *hoof* to either *hoofs* or *hooves*, and some form regular plurals unchanged, as *roof* to *roofs*.

Some irregular plural forms are the original foreign plural forms of words adopted into English, for example *stimuli* from *stimulus*, *phenomena* from *phenomenon*, *criteria* from *criterion*, *larvae* from *larva*. In modern usage there is a growing tendency to anglicize the plural forms of foreign words. Many of these coexist with the plural form, for example *thesauruses* and *thesauri*, *formulas* and *formulae*, *gateaus* and *gateaux* and *indexes* and *indices*. Sometimes the anglicized plural formed according to the regular English rules differs slightly in meaning from the irregular foreign plural. Thus, *indexes* usually applies to guides in books and *indices* is usually used in mathematics.

Some nouns have irregular plurals in that the plural form and the singular form are the same. These include *sheep*, *grouse* (the game-bird) and *salmon*. Also, some nouns have a regular plural and an irregular plural form. Thus, *brother* has the plural forms *brothers* and *brethren*, although *brethren* is now mainly used in a religious context and is archaic in general English.

Appendix C

Spelling

Many adjectives end in '-able' and many end in '-ible'. There are often spelling problems with such adjectives. The following adjectives are likely to be misspelt.

Some adjectives ending in -able:

abominable	commendable	healable
acceptable	conceivable	hearable
adaptable	definable	immovable
adorable	delectable	impassable
advisable	demonstrable	impeccable
agreeable	dependable	implacable
amiable	desirable	impracticable
approachable	discreditable	impressionable
available	disreputable	indescribable
bearable	durable	indispensable
beatable	enviable	inimitable
believable	excitable	insufferable
blameable	excusable	lamentable
calculable	expendable	manageable
capable	foreseeable	measurable
changeable	forgettable	memorable
comfortable	forgivable	nameable

non-flammable   reputable   variable
objectionable   sizeable   viable
operable   stoppable   washable
palpable   tenable   wearable
pleasurable   tolerable   winnable
preferable   transferable   workable
readable   understandable
recognizable   undoable
regrettable   unmistakable
renewable   usable

Some adjectives ending in -ible:

accessible   divisible   perceptible
admissible   edible   permissible
audible   exhaustible   possible
collapsible   expressible   repressible
combustible   fallible   reproducible
compatible   feasible   resistible
comprehensible   flexible   responsible
contemptible   forcible   reversible
credible   gullible   risible
defensible   indelible   sensible
destructible   intelligible   susceptible
digestible   irascible   tangible
discernible   negligible   visible

Some words that are difficult to spell
A
abbreviation   abysmal   accessible
abscess   abysmally   accessories
absence   accelerator   accommodate

accompaniment
accumulate
accurate
accustomed
ache
achieve
aching
acknowledge
acknowledgement/
acknowledgment
acquaint
acquaintance
acquiesce
acquiescence
acquire
acquit
acquittal
acquitted
acreage
across
actual
additional
additive
address
adequate
adieu
adjacent
admissible
admittance
adolescence
adolescent

advantageous
advertisement
advice
advise
aerate
aerial
aesthetic
affect
affiliation
afforestation
aggravate
aggravation
aggregate
aggression
aggressive
aghast
agnosticism
agoraphobia
agreeable
agreeably
agreed
aisle
alcohol
alfresco
alibis
align
alignment
allege
allergic
alleys
alligator

allocate
allotment
allotted
almond
alms
alphabetically
already
although
aluminium
ambiguous
amethyst
ammunition
anachronism
anaesthetic
analyse
analysis
anarchist
ancestor
ancestry
anemone
angrily
anguish
annihilate
annihilation
anniversary
announcement
annulled
annulment
anonymous
anorak
anorexia

answered
Antarctic
antibiotic
antithesis
anxiety
apartheid
apologize
appalling
apparently
appearance
appendicitis
appreciate
approval
aquarium
aquiline
arbiter
arbitrary
arbitration
archaeology
architectural
Arctic
arguably
arrangement
arrival
arthritis
artichoke
ascend
ascent
asphalt
asphyxiate
asphyxiation

assassin
assassinate
assessment
assistance
associate
asthma
asthmatic
astrakhan
atheist
atrocious
attach
attendant
attitude
aubergine
auburn
auctioneer
audible
aural
automatic
autumn
awful
awkward

B
bachelor
bagatelle
baggage
bailiff
ballast
ballerina
balloted

banana
banister
bankruptcy
banquet
barbecue
barometer
barrister
basically
basis
bassoon
battalion
bazaar
beautiful
befriend
beguile
behaviour
beleaguer
belief
believe
belligerent
benefited
bequeath
berserk
besiege
bettered
bevelled
bewitch
bias
bicycle
biennial
bigamous

bigoted
bilingual
biscuit
bivouacked
blancmange
blasphemous
blasphemy
bleary
blitz
bodily
bonfire
bootee
borough
bouquet
bourgeois
boutique
bracketed
Braille
brassiere
breadth
Breathalyzer
brief
broccoli
brochure
bronchitis
bruise
brusque
buccaneer
Buddhist
budding
budgerigar

budgeted
buffeted
bulimia
bulletin
bumptious
bungalow
buoyancy
buoyant
bureau
bureaucracy
business
buttoned

C

cabbage
cafeteria
caffeine
camouflage
campaign
campaigned
cancelled
cancerous
candour
cannabis
cannibal
canvassing
capability
capillary
capitalist
caravan
carbohydrate

carburettor
career
caress
caries
carriage
cartoonist
cashier
cassette
castanets
casualty
catalogue
catarrh
catechism
catering
cauliflower
cautious
ceiling
cellophane
cemetery
centenary
centilitre
centimetre
certainty
champagne
championed
chancellor
changeable
channelled
characteristic
chasm
chauffeur

cheetah
cherish
chief
chilblain
chintz
chiropody
chisel
cholesterol
choreographer
choreography
chronically
chrysanthemum
cigarette
cinnamon
circuitous
cistern
civilian
claustrophobia
clientele
clique
coalesce
cocoa
coconut
coffee
cognac
coincidence
colander
collaborate
collapsible
colleague
colonel

coloration
colossal
comically
commandeer
commemorate
commentator
commercial
commiserate
commission
commissionaire
commissioner
commitment
committal
committed
committee
communicate
commuter
companion
comparative
comparison
compatibility
compelled
competitive
computer
computerization
conceal
concealment
conceit
conceive
concession
concurrent

concussion
condemned
condescend
confectionery
conference
confetti
congeal
congratulations
conjunctivitis
conned
connoisseur
conscience
conscientious
conscious
consequently
consignment
consolation
conspicuous
constitute
consumer
contemptible
continent
continuous
contraception
contradictory
controlled
controller
controversial
convalesce
convenient
convertible

conveyed
convolvulus
coolly
co-operate
co-operative
co-ordinate
copying
co-respondent
coquette
corduroy
coronary
correspondence
corridor
corroborate
corrugated
cosmopolitan
cosseted
councillor
counselling
counterfeit
courageous
courteous
crèche
credible
credited
crematorium
creosote
crescent
crisis
criterion
crocheted

crocodile
croupier
crucial
crucifixion
cruelly
cruise
cryptic
cubicle
cupful
curable
curiosity
curious
currency
curriculum vitae
customary
cynic
cynicism
cynosure

D

dachshund
daffodil
dahlia
dais
damage
dandruff
darkened
debatable
debauched
debility
deceased

deceit
deceive
deciduous
decipher
decoyed
decrease
decreed
defamatory
defeat
defendant
defied
definite
definitely
dehydrate
deign
deliberate
delicatessen
delicious
delinquent
delirious
demeanour
demonstrate
denouement
denunciation
dependence
depth
derailment
dermatitis
derogatory
descend
descendant

desiccate
desperate
detach
detachable
detergent
deterred
deterrent
deuce
develop
developed
development
diabetes
diagnosis
dialogue
dialysis
diametrically
diaphragm
diarrhoea
difference
different
dilapidated
dilemma
dilettante
diminish
diminution
dinosaur
diphtheria
diphthong
disadvantageous
disagreeable
disagreed

disagreement
disappearance
disappeared
disappoint
disapproval
disastrous
disbelief
disbelieve
discipline
discotheque
discouraging
discourteous
discrepancy
discrimination
discussion
disease
disguise
dishevelled
dishonourable
disillusion
disinfectant
disinherited
dismissal
disobeyed
disparage
dispelled
disposal
dispossess
dissatisfaction
dissatisfy
dissect

disseminate
dissent
dissident
dissimilar
dissipated
dissipation
dissociate
dissolute
dissuade
distilled
distillery
distinguish
distraught
disuse
divisible
documentary
doggerel
domineering
donate
doubt
dragooned
drastically
draughty
drooled
drooped
drunkenness
dubious
dumbfounded
dungarees
duress
dutiful

dynamite
dysentery
dyslexia
dyspepsia

E
eccentric
ecclesiastic
ecologically
economically
ecstasy
eczema
effective
effervescence
efficacious
efficient
effrontery
eightieth
elaborate
electrician
elevenses
eligible
emancipate
embarrass
embarrassment
emergence
emergent
emolument
emotional
emphasize
employee

emptied
enable
encourage
encyclopedia
endeavour
endurance
energetically
enervate
engineer
enough
ensuing
entailed
enthusiasm
enumerate
epilepsy
equalize
equalled
equipped
erroneous
erudite
escalator
escapism
espionage
essence
essential
estranged
etiquette
euthanasia
eventually
evidently
exaggerate

exaggeration
exasperate
exceed
exceedingly
excellent
excessive
exchequer
excommunicate
exercise
exhaust
exhibit
exhilarate
exorcise
explanation
exquisite
extinguish
extraneous
extravagant

F
fabulous
facetious
facsimile
faeces
Fahrenheit
fallacious
fanatic
farcical
fascia
fascinate
fascist

fatigue
fatuous
fax
February
feeler
feign
ferocious
festooned
feud
feudal
fevered
fiasco
fibre
fictitious
fiend
fierce
fiery
filial
finesse
flabbergasted
flaccid
flammable
flannelette
flotation
fluent
fluoridate
fluoride
fluoridize
focal
foliage
forcible

foreigner
forfeit
formative
forthwith
fortieth
fortuitous
fortunately
frailty
frankincense
fraudulent
freedom
freight
frequency
friend
frolicked
fuchsia
fuel
fuelled
fugitive
fulfil
fulfilled
fulfilment
fullness
fulsome
furious
furniture
furthered

G
gaiety
galloped

garrison
garrotted
gases
gateau
gauge
gazetteer
geisha
generator
genuine
gerbil
gesticulate
ghastly
ghetto
gigantic
gingham
giraffe
glamorous
glamour
glimpse
global
gluttonous
glycerine
gnarled
gnash
goitre
gossiped
government
graffiti
grammar
grandeur
gratefully

gratitude
gratuitous
greetings
gregarious
grief
grieve
grovelled
gruesome
guarantee
guarantor
guard
guardian
guest
guillotine
guinea
guise
guitar
gymkhana
gynaecology
gypsy/gipsy

H
haemoglobin
haemorrhage
halcyon
hallucination
hammered
handfuls
handicapped
handkerchief
happened

harangue
harass
harlequin
haughty
hazard
hearse
height
heightened
heinous
heir
herbaceous
hereditary
heroism
hesitate
hiccup, hiccough
hideous
hierarchy
hieroglyphics
hijack
hilarious
hindrance
hippopotamus
holiday
holocaust
homeopathy
homoeopathy
homonym
honorary
honour
hooligan
hormonal

hormone
horoscope
horrible
horticulture
hullabaloo
humorous
humour
hurricane
hurried
hygiene
hyphen
hypnosis
hypochondria
hypocrisy
hypothesis
hypothetical
hysterectomy
hysterical

I
icicle
ideological
idiosyncrasy
ignorance
illegible
illegitimate
illiterate
imaginative
imitation
immaculate
immediate

immemorial
immoral
immovable
impasse
impeccable
imperative
imperceptible
imperious
impetuous
impresario
imprisoned
imprisonment
inaccessible
inadmissible
inappropriate
inaugural
incandescent
incessant
incipient
incognito
incommunicado
inconceivable
incongruous
incontrovertible
incorrigible
incredulous
incriminate
incubator
incurred
indefatigable
indefinable

indefinite
independence
independent
indescribable
indict
indictment
indigenous
indigestible
indomitable
indubitable
ineligible
inescapable
inexcusable
inexhaustible
infallible
infatuated
inferred
infinitive
inflamed
inflammable
inflationary
ingratiate
ingredient
inhabitant
inheritance
inhibition
iniquitous
initiate
initiative
innate
innocuous

innumerable
innumerate
inoculate
insecticide
inseparable
insincere
insistence
instalment
instantaneous
intercept
interference
interior
intermediate
intermittent
interpret
interpretation
interrogate
interrupt
interview
intrigue
intrinsically
intuition
intuitive
invariably
inveigle
inveterate
involuntary
involvement
irascible
irrelevant
irreparable

irreplaceable
irresistible
irresponsible
irrevocable
irritable
italicize
itinerant
itinerary

J
jackal
jeopardize
jettisoned
jewellery
jodhpurs
juggernaut
jugular

K
kaleidoscopic
karate
keenness
khaki
kidnapped
kilometre
kiosk
kitchenette
kleptomania
knick-knack
knowledgeable
kow-tow

L
labelled
laboratory
labyrinth
lackadaisical
laddered
lager
language
languor
languorous
laryngitis
larynx
lassitude
latitude
laundered
launderette
layette
league
leanness
ledger
legendary
legible
legitimate
length
lengthened
leukaemia
levelled
liaise
liaison
lieu
lieutenant

lilac
limousine
lineage
linen
lingerie
linguist
liqueur
literature
litre
livelihood
loneliness
loosened
loquacious
lorgnette
lucrative
lucre
luggage
lugubrious
luminous
luscious
lustre
luxurious
lyric

M
macabre
maelstrom
magician
magnanimous
mahogany
maintenance

malaise
malaria
malignant
manageable
management
mannequin
manoeuvre
mantelpiece
manually
margarine
marijuana
marquee
martyr
marvellous
marzipan
masochist
massacre
matinee
matriarch
mayonnaise
meagre
measurement
medallion
medieval
mediocre
melancholy
meningitis
meringue
messenger
meteorological
metropolitan

microphone
microwave
midday
migraine
mileage
milieu
millionaire
mimicked
mimicry
miniature
miraculous
mirrored
miscellaneous
mischief
mischievous
misogynist
misshapen
misspell
misspent
modelled
modelling
morgue
mortgage
mosquito
mountaineer
moustache
multitudinous
muscle
museum
mysterious
mythical

N

naive
narrative
naughty
nausea
nautical
necessary
necessity
negligence
negligible
negotiate
neighbourhood
neither
neurotic
neutral
niche
niece
ninetieth
ninth
nocturnal
nonentity
notably
noticeably
notoriety
nuance
numbered
numerate
numerous
nutrient
nutritious

O

obedient
obese
obituary
oblige
oblique
oblivious
obnoxious
obscene
obscenity
obsessive
obstetrician
occasion
occupancy
occupier
occupying
occurred
occurrence
octogenarian
odour
offence
offered
official
officious
ominous
omission
omitted
oncology
oneself
opaque
ophthalmic

opinion
opponent
opportunity
opposite
orchestra
ordinary
original
orthodox
orthopaedic
oscillate
ostracize
outlying
outrageous
overdraft
overrate
overreach
overwrought
oxygen

P

pacifist
paediatrician
paedophile
pageant
pamphlet
panacea
panegyric
panicked
papered
parachute
paradigm

paraffin
paragraph
paralyse
paralysis
paraphernalia
parcelled
parliament
paroxysm
parquet
partially
participant
particle
partner
passenger
passers-by
pastime
patterned
pavilion
peaceable
peculiar
pejorative
pencilled
penicillin
peppered
perceive
perennial
perilous
permissible
permitted
pernicious
perpetrate

persistence
personnel
persuasion
perusal
pessimism
pessimistically
pesticide
phantom
pharmacy
pharyngitis
pharynx
phenomenon
phial
phlegm
physician
physiotherapist
picketed
picnic
picnicked
picturesque
pioneered
pious
piteous
pitiful
plaintiff
plausible
pleurisy
pneumonia
poignant
politician
pollution

polythene
porridge
portrait
portray
positive
possession
possibility
posthumous
potato
potatoes
precede
precedent
precinct
precipice
precocious
preference
preferred
prejudice
preliminary
prepossessing
prerequisite
prerogative
prescription
presence
preservative
prestige
prestigious
pretentious
prevalent
priest
primitive

privatization
privatize
procedure
proceed
procession
professional
profiteering
prohibit
promiscuous
pronunciation
propeller
proposal
proprietor
prosecute
protagonist
protein
provocation
prowess
psalm
psalmist
pseudonym
pseudonymous
psyche
psychiatric
psychic
psychoanalyse
psychology
publicly
pursuit
putative
pyjamas

Q
quarrelsome
questionnaire
queue
quintet

R
rabies
radioed
radios
railing
rancour
ransack
rapist
rapturous
reassurance
rebelled
rebellious
recalcitrant
receipt
receive
recommend
reconnaissance
reconnoitre
recruitment
recurrence
redundant
referee
reference
referred
regatta

regrettable
regretted
rehabilitation
reign
relevant
relief
relieve
reminisce
reminiscence
remuneration
rendezvous
repertoire
repetitive
reprieve
reprisal
requisite
rescind
resemblance
reservoir
resistance
resourceful
responsibility
restaurant
restaurateur
resurrection
resuscitate
retrieve
reunion
reveille
revelry
revenue

reversible
rhapsody
rheumatism
rhododendron
rhyme
rhythm
ricochet
righteous
rigorous
rigour
risotto
riveted
rogue
roughage
roulette
royalty
rucksack
ruinous
rummage
rumour

S
sabotage
sacrilege
saddened
salmon
salvage
sanctuary
sandwich
sanitary
sapphire

satellite
scaffolding
scandalous
scenic
sceptre
schedule
scheme
schizophrenic
schooner
sciatica
science
scissors
scruple
scrupulous
scurrilous
scythe
secretarial
secretary
sedative
sedentary
sensitive
separate
sergeant
serrated
serviceable
serviette
settee
shampooed
shattered
sheikh
sheriff

shield
shovelled
shuddered
siege
significant
silhouette
simply
simultaneous
sincerely
sixtieth
skeleton
skilful
slanderous
slaughter
sleigh
sleight of hand
sluice
smattering
smithereens
snivelled
soccer
solemn
solicitor
soliloquy
soloist
sombre
somersault
sophisticated
sovereign
spaghetti
spectre

spherical
sphinx
sponsor
spontaneity
spontaneous
squabble
squandered
squawk
staccato
staggered
stammered
statistics
statutory
stealth
stereophonic
stirrup
storage
strait-laced
straitjacket
strategic
strength
strenuous
stupor
suave
subpoena
subtle
succeed
successful
successor
succinct
succulent

succumb
suddenness
suede
sufficient
suffocate
suicide
sullenness
summoned
supercilious
superfluous
supersede
supervise
supervisor
supplementary
surgeon
surveillance
surveyor
susceptible
suspicious
sycamore
symmetry
sympathize
symphony
synagogue
syndicate
synonym
syringe

T

tableau
taboo

taciturn
taffeta
tangerine
tangible
targeted
tattoo
technique
teenager
televise
temperature
tenuous
terrifically
terrifying
territory
terrorist
therapeutic
therefore
thief
thinness
thirtieth
thorough
thoroughfare
threshold
thrombosis
throughout
thwart
thyme
tightened
titillate
titivate
tobacconist

toboggan
toffee
tomato
tomatoes
tomorrow
tonsillitis
topsy-turvy
tornadoes
torpedoes
torpor
tortoiseshell
tortuous
totalled
tourniquet
towelling
traffic
trafficked
tragedy
traitorous
tranquillity
tranquillizer
transcend
transferable
transferred
transparent
travelled
traveller
tremor
triggered
trilogy
troublesome

trousseau
truism
trustee
tsetse
tuberculosis
tumour
tunnelled
tureen
turquoise
twelfth
tyranny

U

unanimous
unconscious
undoubted
unduly
unequalled
unique
unnecessary
unprecedented
unremitting
unrequited
unrivalled
upheaval
uproarious

V

vaccinate
vacuum
vague

variegate
vegan
vehement
vendetta
veneer
ventilator
verandah or
veranda
vermilion
veterinary
vetoes
vice versa
vicissitude
videoed
vigorous
vigour
viscount
visibility
vivacious
vociferous
voluminous
volunteered
vulnerable

W

walkie-talkie
walloped
weakened
wearisome
Wednesday
weight

weird
whereabouts
wherewithal
whinge
widened
width
wield
wintry
witticism
wizened
woebegone
wooden
woollen
worsened
worship
worshipped
wrapper
wrath
wreak
writhe

X

xylophone

Y

yield
yoghurt

Z

zealous
zigzagged

Some words with totally different meanings have similar spellings and therefore can be easily confused

aboard	affluent	alteration
abroad	effluent	altercation
accept	ail	alternately
except	ale	alternatively
access	air	amateur
excess	heir	amateurish
acme	all	amend
acne	awl	emend
ad	allay	amiable
add	alley	amicable
adapter	allegory	among
adaptor	allergy	between
addition	alley	amoral
edition	allay	immoral
	alliterate	immortal
adverse	illiterate	angel
averse		angle
	allude	
advice	elude	annals
advise		annuals
	allusion	
aesthetic	delusion	annex
ascetic	illusion	annexe
affect	altar	annuals
effect	alter	annals

antiquated	awl	base
antique	all	bass
arc	axes	bated
ark	axis	baited
arisen	bad	bath
arose	bade	bathe
artist	bade	baton
artiste	bid	batten
ascent	bail	bawl
assent	bale	ball
ascetic	bale out	bazaar
aesthetic	baited	bizarre
assay	bated	beach
essay	ball	beech
assent	bawl	bean
ascent	ballet	been
astrology	ballot	being
astronomy	banns	beat
ate	bans	beet
eaten	bare	beau
aural	bear	bow
oral	barn	became
averse	baron	become
adverse	barren	beech
		beach

been
bean
being

beer
bier

beet
beat

befallen
befell

began
begun

being
bean
been

belief
believe

bell
belle

bellow
below

beret
berry
bury

berth
birth

beside
besides

between
among

bid
bade

bier
beer

bight
bite

birth
berth

bit
bitten

bite
bight

bizarre
bazaar

blew
blown

blew
blue

bloc
block

blond
blonde

blown
blew

blue
blew

boar
boor

bore
board
bored

boast
boost

bonny
bony

bookie
bouquet

boor
boar
bore

boost
boast

bootee
booty

bore	brassière	brooch
boar	brazier	broach
boor	bray	buffet
bore	brae	[buffit]
born	brazier	buffet
borne	brassière	[boofa]
borough	breach	buoy
burgh	breech	boy
bough	bread	burgh
bow	bred	borough
bound	break	beret
bounded	brake	berry
bouquet	breath	but
bookie	breathe	butt
blow	bred	buy
beau	bread	by
		bye
bow	breech	
bough	breach	cache
		cash
boy	bridal	
buoy	bridle	caddie
		caddy
brae	broach	
bray	brooch	calf
		calve
brake	broke	
break	broken	callous
		callus

calve	cast	cheap
calf	caste	cheep
came	cavalier	check
come	cavalry	cheque
canned	ceiling	checked
could	sealing	chequered
cannon	cell	cheep
canon	sell	cheap
can't	cellular	cheque
cant	cellulose	check
canvas	censor	chilli
canvass	censure	chilly
carat	cent	choir
carrot	scent	quire
	sent	
cart	centenarian	choose
kart	centenary	chose
		chosen
cartilage	cereal	
cartridge	serial	chord
carton	chafe	cord
cartoon	chaff	chose
cartridge	charted	choose
cartilage	chartered	chosen
cash	chased	chute
cache	chaste	shoot

cite
sight
site

clothes
cloths

coarse
course

collage
college

coma
comma

come
came

comma
coma

commissionaire
commissioner

complement
compliment

complementary
complimentary

concert
consort

confidant
confidante
confident

conscience
conscientious
conscious

consort
concert

consul
council
counsel

continual
continuous

coop
coup

coral
corral

cord
chord

co-respondent
correspondent

cornet
coronet

cornflour
cornflower

coronet
cornet

corps
corpse

corral
coral

correspondent
co-respondent

cost
costed

could
canned

council
counsel
consul

councillor
counsellor

coup
coop

course
coarse

courtesy
curtsy

creak
creek

crevasse
crevice

crochet
crotchet

cue
queue

curb
kerb

currant
current

curtsy
courtesy

cygnet
signet

cymbal
symbol

dairy
diary

dam
damn

dammed
damned

damn
dam

dear
deer

decry
descry

deer
dear

delusion
allusion
illusion

dependant
dependent

deprecate
depreciate

descendant
descendent

descry
decry

desert
dessert

device
devise

devolution
evolution

dew
due

diary
dairy

did
done

die
dye

died
dyed

dinghy
dingy

disbelief
disbelieve

discus
discuss

doe
dough

doily
dolly

done
did

dough
doe

draft
draught

dragon	dully	eerie
dragoon	duly	eyrie
draught	dungeon	effect
draft	dudgeon	affect
drawn	dux	effluent
drew	ducks	affluent
drank	dye	elder
drunk	die	eldest
drew	dyed	elicit
drawn	died	illicit
driven	dyeing	eligible
drove	dying	legible
drunk	earthly	ellipse
drank	earthy	eclipse
dual	easterly	elude
duel	eastern	allude
ducks	eaten	emend
dux	ate	amend
dudgeon	eclipse	emigrant
dungeon	ellipse	immigrant
due	economic	emigration
dew	economical	immigration
Jew		
duel	edition	emission
dual	addition	omission

emphasis	etymologist	expiate
emphasize	entomologist	expatiate
employee	evolution	extant
employer	devolution	extinct
ensure	ewe	eyrie
insure	yew	eerie
entomologist	you	faerie
etymologist	except	fairy
envelop	accept	fain
envelope	excess	feign
epigram	access	faint
epitaph	executioner	feint
epithet	executor	fair
ere	exercise	fare
err	exorcise	fairy
erotic	expand	faerie
erratic	expend	fallen
err	expansive	fell
ere	expensive	felled
erratic	expatiate	fare
erotic	expiate	fair
escapement	expend	fate
escarpment	expand	fête
essay	expensive	faun
assay	expansive	fawn

feat	flammable	flown
feet	inflammable	flew
feign	flare	flue
fain	flair	flew
feint	flea	foment
faint	flee	ferment
fell	flew	font
fallen	flu	fount
felled		
	flue	forbade
ferment	flew	forbidden
foment	flown	
		fore
fête	flocks	four
fate	phlox	
		foregone
fiancé	floe	forgone
fiancée	flow	
		foresaw
filed	flour	foreseen
filled	flower	
		foreword
final	floury	forward
finale	flowery	
		forgave
fir	flow	forgiven
fur	flow	
		forgone
fission	flower	foregone
fissure	flour	
		forgone
flair	flowery	forwent
flare	floury	

forgot	four	gamble
forgotten	fore	gambol
forsaken	fourth	gaol
forsook	forth	goal
forswore	fowl	gate
forsworn	foul	gait
fort	franc	gave
forte	frank	given
forty		
	freeze	genie
forth	frieze	genius
fourth		genus
	froze	
forty	frozen	genteel
fort		gentile
forte	funeral	gentle
	funereal	
forward		genus
foreword	fur	genie
	fir	genius
forwent		
forgone	gabble	gild
	gable	guild
foul		
fowl	gaff	gilt
	gaffe	guilt
found		
founded	gait	given
	gate	gave
fount	galleon	glacier
font	gallon	glazier

goal
gaol

gone
went

gorilla
guerrilla

gourmand
gourmet

gradation
graduation

grate
great

grew
grown

grief
grieve

grill
grille

griped
gripped

grisly
gristly
grizzly

grope
group

ground
grounded

grown
grew

guerrilla
gorilla

guild
gild

guilt
gilt

hail
hale

hair
hare

half
halve

hallo
hallow
halo

halve
half

hangar
hanger

hanged
hung

hanger
hangar

hare
hair

hart
heart

heal
heel

hear
here

heart
hart

heel
heal

heir
air

here
hear

heron
herring

hew
hue

hewed
hewn

hid	horse	immigration
hidden	hoarse	emigration
higher	hue	immoral
hire	hew	amoral
		immortal
him	human	
hymn	humane	immorality
		immortality
hire	humiliation	
higher	humility	impetuous
		impetus
hoar	hung	
whore	hanged	impracticable
		impractical
hoard	hymn	
horde	him	inapt
		inept
hoarse	idle	
horse	idol	incredible
		incredulous
hole	illegible	
whole	ineligible	indigenous
		indigent
honorary	illicit	
honourable	elicit	industrial
		industrious
hoop	illiterate	
whoop	alliterate	ineligible
		illegible
hoped	illusion	
hopped	allusion	inept
	delusion	inapt
horde		
hoard	immigrant	inflammable
	emigrant	flammable

ingenious	kerb	known
ingenuous	curb	knew
inhuman	key	lade
inhumane	quay	laid
insure	knave	lay
ensure	nave	lied
intelligent	knead	lain
intelligible	kneed	lane
interment	need	
internment	knew	lair
	known	layer
invertebrate		
inveterate	knew	lama
	new	llama
jam		
jamb	knight	lane
	night	lain
Jew		
dew	knightly	laterally
due	nightly	latterly
jib	knit	lath
jibe	nit	lathe
judicial	knot	latterly
judicious	not	laterally
junction	knotty	lay
juncture	naughty	lade
kart	know	laid
cart	no	lied

layer	liar	loath
lair	lyre	loathe
lea	libel	local
lee	liable	locale
lead	licence	lode
led	license	load
leak	lied	lone
leek	lade	loan
led	laid	looped
lead	lay	loped
		lopped
lee	lightening	
lea	lightning	loose
		lose
leek	lineament	
leak	liniment	loot
		lute
legible	liqueur	
eligible	liquor	loped
		lopped
lemming	literal	looped
lemon	literary	
	literate	lose
leopard		loose
leper	llama	
	lama	loth
lessen		loathe
lesson	load	
	lode	lumbar
liable		lumber
libel	loan	
	lone	

lute	manner	meat
loot	manor	meet
		mete out
lyre	mare	
liar	mayor	medal
		meddle
macaroni	marina	
macaroon	merino	mediate
		meditate
made	marshal	
maid	martial	meet
		meat
magnate	marten	mete out
magnet	martin	
		merino
maid	martial	marina
made	marshal	
		metal
mail	martin	mettle
male	marten	
		mete out
main	mask	meat
mane	masque	meet
maize	mat	meter
maze	matt	metre
male	mayor	mettle
mail	mare	metal
mane	maze	mews
main	maize	muse
maniac	mean	mien
manic	mien	mean

might	moral	naughty
mite	morale	knotty
miner	morality	naval
minor	mortality	navel
minister	mote	nave
minster	moat	knave
missal	motif	navel
missile	motive	naval
mistaken	mouse	navvy
mistook	moose	navy
	mousse	
mite		nay
might	mucous	née
	mucus	neigh
moat		
mote	multiple	need
	multiply	knead
modal		kneed
model	muscle	
module	mussel	negligent
		negligible
momentary	muse	
momentous	mews	neigh
momentum		nay
	mussel	née
moose	muscle	
mouse		net
mousse	mystic	nett
	mystique	
moped		new
mopped	naught	knew
	nought	

night	omission	pain
knight	emission	pane
nightly	oral	pair
knightly	aural	pare
		pear
nit	ore	
knit	oar	palate
		palette
no	organism	pallet
know	orgasm	
		pale
northerly	outdid	pail
northern	outdone	
		palette
not	overcame	palate
knot	overcome	pallet
nougat	overdid	pane
nugget	overdone	pain
nought	overran	par
naught	overrun	parr
nugget	overtaken	pare
nougat	overtook	pear
		pair
oar	overthrew	
ore	overthrown	parr
		par
of	packed	
off	pact	passed
		past
official	pail	
officious	pale	

pastel
pastille

pate
pâté
patty

peace
piece

peak
peek
pique

peal
peel

pear
pair
pare

pearl
purl

peasant
pheasant

pedal
peddle

peek
peak
pique

peel
peal

peer
pier

pence
pennies

pendant
pendent

pennies
pence

perquisite
prerequisite

personal
personnel

petrel
petrol

pheasant
peasant

phlox
flocks

piazza
pizza

piece
peace

pier
peer

pined
pinned

piped
pipped

pique
peak
peek

pistil
pistol

pizza
piazza

place
plaice

plain
plane

plaintiff
plaintive

plait
plate

plane
plain

plate
plait

plum	precede	program
plumb	proceed	programme
politic	premier	proof
political	première	prove
pool	prerequisite	property
pull	perquisite	propriety
poplar	prey	prophecy
popular	pray	prophesy
pore	price	prophet
pour	prise	profit
	prize	
pored		propriety
poured	principal	property
	principle	
poser		prostate
poseur	prise	prostrate
	price	
pour	prize	prove
pore		proof
	private	
poured	privet	pull
pored		pool
	prize	
practicable	prise	purl
practical	price	pearl
practice	proceed	put
practise	precede	putt
pray	profit	quash
prey	prophet	squash

quay
key

queue
cue

quiet
quite

quire
choir

quite
quiet

racket
racquet

radar
raider

raged
ragged

raider
radar

rain
reign
rein

raise
raze

rampant
rampart

ran
run

rang
ringed
rung

rap
wrap

raped
rapped

rapped
rapt
wrapped

rated
ratted

raze
raise

read
red

read
reed

real
reel

red
read

reel
real

refuge
refugee

regal
regale

reign
rain
rein

relief
relieve

reproof
reprove

respectful
respective

rest
wrest

retch
wretch

review
revue

rhyme
rime

ridden
rode

right   rose   sang
rite   risen   sung

               rote   sank
rime   wrote   sunk
rhyme   sunken
               rough
ring   ruff   saviour
wring   savour
               rout
ringed   route   saw
rang   seen
rung   row
               roe   sawed
risen   sawn
rose   rowed
               road   scared
rite   rode   scarred
right
write   ruff   scene
               rough   seen
road
rode   run   scent
rowed   ran   cent
                              sent
rode   rung
ridden   wrung   sceptic
                              septic
roe   rye
row   wry   scraped
                              scrapped
rôle   sail
roll   sale   sculptor
                              sculpture
               salon
               saloon

sea	sensual	sextant
see	sensuous	sexton
sealing	sent	shaken
ceiling	scent	shook
	cent	
seam		shear
seem	septic	sheer
	sceptic	
sear		sheared
seer	sere	sheered
sere	sear	shorn
	seer	
secret		shelf
secrete	serial	shelve
	cereal	
see		shoe
sea	series	shoo
	serious	
seem		shook
seam	sew	shaken
	so	
seen	sow	shoot
saw		chute
	sewed	
seen	sewn	shorn
scene		sheared
	sewer	sheered
seer	sower	
sear		showed
sere	sewn	shown
	sewed	
sell		shrank
cell	sewn	shrunk
	sown	

sight	sloe	soot
cite	slow	suit
site		
	sloped	sore
signet	slopped	soar
cygnet		
	slow	soul
silicon	sloe	sole
silicone		
	smelled	southerly
singeing	smelt	southern
singing		
	sniped	sow
sinuous	snipped	sew
sinus		so
	so	
site	sew	sowed
cite	sow	sown
sight		
	soar	sower
skies	sore	sewer
skis		
	sociable	sown
slain	social	sewn
slew		
	solder	spared
slated	soldier	sparred
slatted		
	sole	speciality
slay	soul	specialty
sleigh		
	some	species
slew	sum	specious
slain		
	son	sped
	sun	speeded

spoke	statue	straightened
spoken	statute	straitened
sprang	staunch	stratum
sprung	stanch	stratus
squash	stayed	strewed
quash	staid	strewn
staid	steak	strife
stayed	stake	strive
stair	steal	striped
stare	steel	stripped
stake	step	strive
steak	steppe	strife
stalk	stile	striven
stock	style	strove
stanch	stimulant	stunk
staunch	stimulus	stank
stank	stock	sty
stunk	stalk	stye
stare	stocked	style
stair	stoked	stile
stared	storey	suede
starred	story	swede
stationary	straight	suit
stationery	strait	soot

suite	swelled	tapped
sweet	swollen	taped
sum	swingeing	tare
some	swinging	tear
summary	swollen	taught
summery	swelled	taut
sun	swore	tax
son	sworn	tacks
sundae	swum	tea
Sunday	swam	tee
sung	symbol	team
sang	cymbal	teem
sunk	tacks	tear
sank	tax	tare
sunken		
super	tail	tear
supper	tale	tier
surplice	taken	tee
surplus	took	tea
swam	tale	teem
swum	tail	team
swede	taped	teeth
suede	tapped	teethe
sweet	taper	temporal
suite	tapir	temporary

tendon
tenon

tenor
tenure

testimonial
testimony

their
there
they're

thorough
through

thrash
thresh

threw
through

threw
thrown

throes
throws

throne
thrown

through
thorough

through
threw

thrown
throne

throws
throes

thyme
time

tic
tick

tier
tear

tiled
tilled

timber
timbre

time
thyme

tire
tyre

to
too
two

toe
tow

tomb
tome

ton
tonne
tun

too
to
two

took
taken

topi
toupee

tore
torn

tow
toe

trait
tray

treaties
treatise

trod
trodden

troop
troupe

tun
ton
tonne

turban

turbine

two

to

too

tycoon

typhoon

tyre

tire

unaware

unawares

unconscionable

unconscious

undid

undone

unwanted

unwonted

urban

urbane

vacation

vocation

vain

vane

vein

vale

veil

venal

venial

veracity

voracity

vertex

vortex

vigilant

vigilante

vocation

vacation

voracity

veracity

vortex

vertex

wafer

waver

waged

wagged

waif

waive

wave

waist

waste

want

wont

warden

warder

ware

wear

waste

waist

wave

waif

waive

waver

wafer

way

weigh

weak

week

wear

ware

weekly

weakly

weigh

way

went

gone

westerly
western

wet
whet

whit
wit

whole
hole

whoop
hoop

whore
hoar

willed
would

winded
wound

wit
whit

withdrawn
withdrew

wittily
wittingly

woe
woo

woke
woken

wont
want

woo
woe

wore
worn

would
willed

would
wood
wooed

wove
woven

wrap
rap

wrapped
rapped
rapt

wreak
wreck

wreath
wreathe

wrest
rest

wretch
retch

wring
ring

write
right
rite

wrote
rote

wrote
written

wrung
rung

wry
rye

yew
ewe
you

yoke
yolk

yore
your